# Therapist as Life Coach

# THERAPIST AS LIFE COACH
## *An Introduction for Counselors and Other Helping Professionals*

REVISED AND EXPANDED

## Patrick Williams
## and Deborah C. Davis

W. W. Norton & Company

New York • London

For information about permission to reproduce
selections from this book, write to:
Permissions, W. W. Norton & Company, Inc.,
500 Fifth Avenue, New York, NY 10110

Production Manager: Leeann Graham
Manufacturing by Quebecor World Fairfield Graphics

**Library of Congress Cataloging-in-Publication Data**

Williams, Patrick, 1950–
   Therapist as life coach : an introduction for counselors and other
helping professionals / Patrick Williams and Deborah C. Davis. -- Rev.
and expanded
     p.   cm.
"A Norton professional book."
Includes bibliographical references and index.
**ISBN 978-0-393-70522-5** (hardcover)
   I. Personal coaching 2. Counseling psychology. 3. Conduct of life.
   I. Davis, Deborah C. II. Title.

BF637.P36.W545 2007
158'.3--dc22                                                    2007020123

W. W. Norton & Company, Inc., 500 fifth Avenue, New York, N.Y. 10110
www.wwnorton.com

W. W. Norton & Company Ltd., Castle House, 75/76 Wells St., London WIT 3QT

1   3   5   7   9   0   8   6   4   2

# Contents

# Acknowledgments

Many people have influenced our book. We recognize, after working for years in the helping professions as practitioners and teachers, that the fabric of who we are and what we say today is a composite of the many people who have touched us along the way. We've learned from clients, teachers, counselors, coaches, and many other wise individuals. We thank all of them for their wonderful contributions to our lives.

Throughout our book we've made a good faith effort to give credit to those who originally created the information we share. Some of the quotes we have included are part of collections we've maintained for years. We hope that you enjoy them as we did, and that we've truly given all recognition where it is due.

We especially want to acknowledge certain individuals for their contributions to the coaching profession and to this book. To Dave Ellis, Laura Berman Fortgang, Peter Reding, Frederic Hudson, Thomas Leonard, Sir John Whitmore, Sherry Lowry, Diane Menendez, Julio Olalla, Cheryl Richardson, Sandy Vilas, Laura Whitworth, and Henry Kimsey-House, we offer our deepest respect and appreciation for their support and pioneering spirit in creating the momentum for the profession of life coaching.

We also thank Deborah Malmud, Director of Norton Professional Books, for her belief in our message to life coaches, her faith in our abilities to deliver the product, and her dedication to seeing that our book achieve the professional level we desire.

This book literally would not be in your hands but for the tireless dedication of Edwina Adams, who prepared our manuscript word by word. She graciously accepted our various forms of writing and helped us find one voice with which to communicate our message. Her dedication and encouragement helped our dream materialize, and we will be forever grateful.

Finally, we dedicate this book to our fathers, Vernon Williams and Raymond D. Davis. These men were our first life coaches, and through their words and deeds we learned to be friendly, open-minded, and willing to laugh at ourselves. They taught us to give whatever we took on in life our full attention and best work. We believe they would have enjoyed our book. We hope you do, too.

# Introduction

*How different our lives are when we really know what is deeply
important to us, and, keeping that picture in mind, we manage
ourselves each day to be and do what really matters most.*
—Stephen R. Covey

The experience of writing this book, like many life coaching sessions, was
eye-opening. It demonstrated what is possible when humans dream, communicate, and strive to achieve that which seemed only a faint and distant goal
in the quiet corners of their minds.

We presented our first joint workshop in October 1998 at a conference
of the American Association of Marriage and Family Therapists. We didn't
know how much participation to expect, even though we sensed that there
was some interest in life coaching. To our delight, over 75 family therapists
filled the room for our presentation and eagerly participated in the discussion. Participants' stories revolved around the theme of wanting something
more out of their helping relationships. They described feeling tired, frustrated, discouraged, and unable to "make a difference" in individual lives the
way they once believed possible. We understood clearly what they were
saying because we both had shared similar feelings and frustrations.

Before we go any further, we'd like to tell you a little bit about our backgrounds and how we came together to write this book.

In the 1970s Pat obtained degrees in humanistic and transpersonal
psychology, which, even then, were not typical courses of study in the field
of psychology. However, he did become a psychologist and actually enjoyed
the work until managed care came along. Before he even realized what had

happened, his clients and the way he did business changed. At first he didn't even realize what was happening, but suddenly it dawned on him that he no longer was working with people who wanted to improve their lives—he was working with people who had one serious mental illness after another. After doing some executive coaching for a while to infuse new energy into his practice, he jumped "feet first" into coaching. He hired a coach, trained at Coach University,* and quickly felt that his heart and soul had found the right place. He subsequently closed his psychology practice and devoted himself full-time to coaching and training therapists interested in becoming coaches.

Deb came to life coaching after being a counselor and family therapist. She spent most of her career as a college counselor, and she taught in a graduate counselor education program. Deb was commended as an exemplary teacher and great mentor for adult learners. In 1994 she noticed the term *coaching* popping up in the literature of the counseling profession, and wondered whether this was just the "helping fad of the month," or whether it might be a legitimate evolution within the helping professions. Deb began using coaching principles with some of her clients and soon found that it was second nature and, more importantly, the principles worked! She read an article by Pat in *Practice Strategies* (the newsletter of the American Association of Marriage and Family Therapy) and contacted him; a lasting and rewarding friendship and professional alliance blossomed. Deb retired from her university professorship in 1999 to focus on teaching and writing about life coaching.

Since we met, we have delivered national presentations on life coaching, collaborated on ideas for the development of the Institute for Life Coach Training curriculum, and discussed more effective ways to share life coaching strategies with helping professionals who want more out of their lives and careers. The book you have before you is a product of our collegial relationship and dedication to training helping professionals to become effective life coaches. We want life coaching to be a household term and a service that is readily available to all who seek it.

Our intuitive belief that helping professionals were ready for a new way to do business has been constantly reinforced over the past several years, as

---

*Coach University, founded by Thomas Leonard in the 1990s, was the first distance-learning-based coach training program.

we have heard from increasing numbers of counselors, psychologists, and family therapists. As we reached out through books, journal articles and presentations, the demand for more information about how therapists could transition into life coaching grew. It was clear that helping professionals wanted something more meaningful and satisfying. We believed that, for many, life coaching could help meet that need.

We wrote this book for therapists considering a career transition into life coaching. In other words, we wrote this book for you. We use the term *therapist* in our book to broadly define helping professionals whose academic preparation and training include areas such as family therapy, psychology, sociology, counseling, and even psychiatry. When we speak of therapists, we want you to know we are speaking to all trained helping professionals.

As you read, you will see that we firmly believe therapists are uniquely positioned to become outstanding life coaches. The transferable helping skills that trained and experienced therapists bring to the coaching relationship are extremely valuable in facilitating successful change and growth in coaching clients. We discuss these skills later in the book, and also address the specific transitions needed in the traditional model of helping in order to create a coaching, rather than therapeutic, relationship.

Although numerous books on the market discuss some aspect of the coaching profession, many of the general coaching publications focus on business or corporate coaching. Our book takes into account the rich history that psychology has to offer, and how professionals with backgrounds and training in the helping professions can transition into a career as a life coach. Additionally, ours is one of the few books with emphasis on the whole-person approach to coaching, which we call life coaching. Whether you are interested in exploring the coaching profession in general as a way to transform your practice, or whether you are specifically focused on life coaching, we believe that you, as a trained helping professional, will find this book a valuable resource to support your transition.

## What Is Life Coaching?

Therapists can renew their souls with life coaching. But what is life coaching? Here are some general definitions from three professional sources:

Life coaches assist people to discover what they want in life and unlock their own brilliance to achieve it. Life coaching is about people generating their own answers, not looking outside of themselves for solutions. This process is not about teaching what you already know or about clients acting as students. Instead, life coaching is empowering people to invent something new—to think something they've never thought before and to say something they've never said before. (Ellis, 1998, pp. 1, 3)

Coaching is a powerful relationship for people making important changes in their lives. (Whitworth, Kimsey-House, & Sandahl, 1998, p. xvii)

Coaching is an ongoing relationship, which focuses on clients taking action toward the realization of their visions, goals, or desires. Coaching uses a process of inquiry and personal discovery to build the client's level of awareness and responsibility and provides the client with structure, support, and feedback. The coaching process helps clients both define and achieve professional and personal goals faster and with more ease than would be possible otherwise. (International Coach Federation, from their website, *www.coachfederation.org*)

How we define life coaching has been the subject of much thought and discussion. As we present workshops across the country, we continue to revise and refine what we believe most captures the essence of life coaching. For us, it is vital that our definition include the following features, all of which we discuss in greater detail later.

- *The focus is on the future.* Life coaching is about designing a future, not getting over a past.
- *The relationship is typically long-term.* Life coaching, using our holistic model, is a relationship that lasts months and years rather than a short-term encounter for a brief, specific concern.

- *The goals, dreams, and visions (wants) drive the action.* Helping clients to discover what they want (in all aspects of their lives) is an essential component of the life coaching relationship.
- *Multiple paths exist to reach each want.* In order to increase the likelihood of success, life coaches help clients create multiple paths to achieve what they want in their lives.
- *The client knows the way* (even though he or she may not realize it at the time). The life coaches we train know that the answers and solutions rest with the client and evolve from the coaching conversation.

Here is our definition of life coaching as it applies to the information we will present. **Life coaching is a powerful human relationship in which trained coaches help people design their future rather than get over their past. Through a typically long-term relationship, coaches aid clients in creating visions and goals for *all* aspects of their lives and multiple strategies to support the achievement of those goals. Coaches recognize their clients' brilliance and their personal power to discover their own solutions when provided with support, accountability, and unconditional positive regard.**

Life coaching can be challenging as well as financially and spiritually rewarding. Making the transition from therapist to life coach requires a journey of self-exploration and self-awareness, as well as creative planning. We recognize from working with many therapists that life coaching is not for everyone. We also know that the therapists who bravely explore this new opportunity often find it to be just what they were seeking in their effort to renew their soul as helpers of the human spirit.

You will get the most out of this book if you actively participate. We've collected stories and quotes from therapists who have become life coaches. As you read them, record your own thoughts, concerns, and insights. We've also designed activities to help you get the most out of your exploration of life coaching. This book can serve as your guide whether life coaching specifically or coaching in general is your goal; we are confident that it provides many opportunities for you to consider new ways of offering your professional helping services.

The life coaching relationship focuses on what the client wants. Similarly, we encourage you to use the time you spend reading our book to consider what you really want in your life. We recognize that it is sometimes hard for helpers to take time to create their own futures, but we really want you to give attention to yourself, your wants, and your desires. Make a commitment to explore, fully and completely, a possible transition into life coaching. Give yourself to the process, clarify your desires, and use effective creative planning. You will be amazed at the results. As you read, think of this question: "What do I want my future as a helping professional to look like, and is life coaching right for me?"

Jeannine Wade, one of the therapists we trained as a life coach through our workshops and the Institute for Life Coach Training* (formerly Therapist University), wrote the following letter. Her words convey her satisfaction in the choice she made and her empowerment from the transition:

> Two years ago, I was becoming aware that I was feeling very "burned out." I felt as though I desperately needed to make some changes, but I didn't know how to begin. I thought, *I don't have enough time for what I need to do now—how can I find the time to make changes?* On the surface, my life was good. I was healthy; I had a nice home, a good husband, and a successful private practice as a psychologist. I had a loving family and friends. But something was missing. And I felt as though I didn't have the time to slow down long enough to figure out what it was. I just knew I felt I had too many responsibilities and not enough time; too many details overwhelming me and I didn't have enough joy and fun. I had not allowed myself the option to make my life better.

---

*The Institute for Life Coach Training, initially Therapist University, was founded by Dr. Patrick Williams in 1998 with the express purpose of providing coach training exclusively to the helping professions. It is one of the premier coach training programs, is internationally recognized, and delivers courses in the United States, Canada, and Europe. ILCT offers a comprehensive training program for the helping professions as well as a certification program.

Then I went to the national meeting of marriage and family therapists in Dallas. The first session I chose to attend was "Adding Coaching to Your Private Practice." I had heard of personal coaching, but I didn't really know what it was.

In that session, two things happened for me. First, I realized that I could change my life for the better—here was someone not only saying it was okay, but also informing me of a whole new field to help me do just that. When I think about it now, it is hard to believe that as much as I was helping others change their lives, I wasn't allowing myself to accept that I could change mine.

And second, I realized that being a part of this new field made me feel excited in a way that I hadn't felt in a long time. It seemed to fit with everything I had been working toward in my life, including the way I did therapy—which is helping individuals to listen to themselves, to believe that they can make their lives better, and to take the steps to make their dreams a reality.

Now, two years later, after hiring my own coach and becoming a coach, my life is very different. I have made many changes that have helped, and I continue to make changes. The biggest change is the belief that I can make my life what I want it to be, and one of my greatest joys is helping others to do the same.

Jeannine represents hundreds of therapists who have made the choice to either add coaching to their therapy business or become full-time life coaches. We'll share more of their stories later on. For now, here is an overview of where we are headed. Part I, "Why Life Coaching?," explores the history of the coaching movement and why we believe society is hungry for life coaches. Part II, "Life Coaching for Therapists," examines similarities and distinctions between coaching and therapy, discusses the coaching relationship, and considers some of the skills therapists will need to learn and unlearn in order to reclaim their joyfulness. Part III, "Powerful Transition Tools," describes getting started as a life coach and the specific tools therapists need in the life coaching relationship and in establishing a successful life coaching practice. Part IV, "Expanding Your Coaching Practice," offers alternatives to the basic life coaching model, offers self-care strategies for life coaches, and peeks into the future of life coaching. Question-and-answer and resources sections follow Part IV.

So, as we move to Part I, remember to sit with that very important question mentioned earlier, "What do I want my future as a helping professional to look like, and is life coaching right for me?"

# Therapist As Life Coach

# ≪ PART I ≫
# Why Life Coaching?

# CHAPTER ONE

# Why Therapists as Life Coaches?

*You see things, and you say, "Why?" But I dream things
that never were; and I say, "Why not?"*
—George Bernard Shaw

Around 1990 there was little mention of coaching except in the corporate culture. Many top managers and CEOs utilized mentoring and executive coaching, either informally from a colleague, or formally by hiring a consultant or psychologist who became their executive coach. We elaborate on the history of coaching more in chapter two, but for now, let us examine why life coaching is becoming more popular and prevalent.

The International Coach Federation, founded in 1992, did not have a real presence until its first convention in 1996. The organization has kept detailed archives of media coverage on coaching since the early 1990s. Two newspaper articles on coaching appeared in 1993, four in 1994 (including one in Australia), and seven in 1995. The majority of articles appeared in publications in the United States. Then, in 1996, a huge increase in publicity occurred, as evidenced by more than 60 articles, television interviews, and radio shows on the topic of coaching. Every year since, media coverage has increased dramatically. This includes live media coverage as well, including national television shows such as *Good Morning America*, Today, and others. This surge in coverage has occurred throughout the United States, Canada Europe, Australia, Africa, Japan, China, and Singapore, as well as other countries.

In addition, the only books written about coaching before the 1990s were geared to corporate and performance coaching. And many books have been published on niches within coaching, such as executive and corporate coaching, leadership, relationship coaching, and parent coaching. One of the most important changes has been the emergence of researched-based published articles and books, which has increased the the acceptance of coaching worldwide in both corporate and academic communities.

Life coaching as a phenomenon originated in the United States and has spread worldwide. Coaching will soon reach a critical mass in society. People will have heard of coaching, know when they need a coach, know how to find a coach, and know the difference between partnering with a life coach and seeking the services of a therapist or counselor.

## Society Is Changing

We believe that this new profession has emerged out of a major shift in societal parameters. Alvin Toffler wrote *Future Shock* in 1970. It was the most popular publication of its time to address the phenomenon of how rapid change impacted the human condition and its societal structures. Toffler's warnings and descriptions seem underestimated in comparison with the exponential speed of change that society now experiences.

We both grew up in the 1950s; at that time, society seemed predictable and stable. People generally stayed married, attended college for four years, and stayed in one career for most or all of their lives. There was little emphasis on adult education, career transitions, or moving far from home or as often as we do today. Company loyalty was big; you worked 30 years or so, got your "gold watch," and had a retirement party. But the times and society have both changed. Now the younger generation's motto is "Have résumé, will travel!" For the baby boomer generation, the trend is to be self-employed or well invested, highly mobile and entrepreneurial.

In the decades before World War II and in the 1950s, there were few therapists or counselors because the profession was just emerging. Now there are well over 500,000 licensed therapists in the United States. In the 1950s, people went to "Uncle Charley," their clergy, or their grandparents for counsel, or they had mentors in the workplace. Today, mentors are not as easily available due to the decrease in lifelong communities—the quiet neighborhoods of the past where everyone knew everyone else, and neighbors, especially older people, served as informal mentors and sages. Constant career changes also have impacted the availability of mentoring.

In the 1970s and 1980s, when corporate America began the great downsizing experiment, the middle manager became a dinosaur to be replaced by work teams, self-management, and trickle-down edicts from executive management. The middle manager had been the mentor, coach, and go-between for employees and the company's top management. As the middle manager disappeared, so did the natural mentoring that was available to employees. People, in both the workplace and in their personal lives, lost their listeners and confidantes. During this period, consultants thrived. Companies hired consultants to offer training packages that gave an outside voice and a seemingly objective ear to address employees' morale issues, absenteeism, conflicts, and relationship struggles in a work team or department. Consultants were viewed as both a necessary evil and a competitive edge.

Today, change is the norm, and both entrepreneurism and isolation, even in a corporate culture, are the result. Additionally, there are more self-employed and home-office workers than ever before, and this trend is growing exponentially. With global communications, virtual technology, e-mail, voice mail, and wireless office technology, we are an entrepreneurial and mobile workforce. In fact, as Judy Feld, a friend and Pat's first coach, wrote in her SOHO Success Letter™ (SOHO stands for Small Office/Home Office) (1998), " . . . growth of the alternative workplace will continue. This is not a fad. Current estimates place 30–40 million people in the USA as either telecommuters or home-based workers." Millions of workers can now conduct their business away from office buildings and can live almost anywhere they choose. This trend has forever changed the traditional nature of the "workplace."


## Why People Need Life Coaches

Society has gone from being stable and mostly predictable to being fast-paced, impersonal, and constantly evolving. As mentioned earlier, with such swift change in all aspects of life and the loss of mentors for most people, life coaching becomes the new profession where an individual can hire a mentor in the form of a personal coach. Carl Rogers once said that psychotherapy was often like "buying a friend"; hiring a coach is a way to buy a mentor and guide and gain the support that otherwise may be difficult to find. Similarly, having a coach has become a sought-after employee benefit in many companies, and for those who are self-employed, a coach can keep them focused, connected to their desired outcomes, and living their life "on purpose."

Many types of coaching are available to people today and, as the profession grows, mental health therapists will be able to fill many specialty niches, such as relationship coaching, parenting coaching, teen coaching, family business coaching, and so on. In the corporate arena, executive coaching is popular and prevalent but often focuses primarily on work goals and work teams, not necessarily whole-life coaching with, as we say, "the person behind the job." Companies are discovering that coaching can lead to more balanced, vibrant, and happy employees, which in turn leads to less turnover, better working relationships, and increased productivity and efficiency. In response to all the pressures from society, and including the lack of stability and predictability, a coach can help the client become what we call a *change master*.

A well-trained and experienced life coach may also refer the client to other coaching specialists, as needed or requested. To be certain, a corporate or executive coach needs special training for the unique challenges of the corporate world, but coaches with other skills also can be used for specific goals. We have referred our individual clients to relationship coaches when they and their spouses needed relationship guidance. Likewise, other coaches (acting as the personal life coach) have made referrals to specialized coaches for clients who needed tips on getting a book published, help with financial planning, or advice on how to deal with an unruly teenager. General life coaching can continue or be resumed after the referral coaching is complete. A life coach is central to the client's life because he or she keeps the client focused, motivated, purposeful, and accountable.

## Why Therapists* Can Make Great Life Coaches

Successful coaches come from a myriad of professional backgrounds. Business and professional consultants, human resources managers, organizational consultants, entrepreneurs, and marketing specialists are a few of the careers that coaches might have had before adding coaching to their résumé. For the purpose of this book, we want to discuss those unique skills that trained and experienced helping professionals bring to life coaching relationships. The following list highlights some of the reasons we believe therapists are uniquely qualified to make the transition into life coaching.

1. *Skillful listening.* Deep and empathic listening is at the heart of the therapeutic relationship, and helping professionals have had much professional experience honing their listening skills. In addition to listening, they are able to hear what is not being said and to detect nuances of expression, voice, and energy that either unite or contradict the client's verbal and nonverbal cues. However, therapists would have to "unlearn" the tendency to analyze and dig into the past in order to be successful coaches.

2. *Gift of reframing.* The skill of putting a positive or less innocuous spin on a statement or belief expressed by a client is critical to effective life coaching. For example, a client might be distraught over not getting her desired promotion. The reframe might be to ask her to consider what she could learn from the experience and to mention that perhaps a greater opportunity will appear in the future. Turning problems into opportunities is one way to use reframing as a coaching skill. Putting the belief into a new "frame" changes the perspective of the statement ,or the belief, toward positive thinking. It's not simply giving it a positive spin. It's also true that clients may have blind spots or a persistent inner critic, and the coach views the situation from outside of that negatively charged perspective.

---

\* Students of the Institute for Life Coach Training have come from many backgrounds. Many are practicing therapists (psychologists, psychotherapists, psychiatrists, marriage and family therapists, social workers) but many others are human resources staff, clergy, trained but unlicensed counselors with agencies or churches, employee assistance professionals, teachers, and other helping professionals who are not professional therapists or counselors but have a background or position that requires basic skills of counseling. ILCT's training is respected as one of the most comprehensive, theory-based, whole-person approaches in the world, and any professional could benefit from the training. The curriculum, however, like this book, is targeted to therapists, counselors, and other helping professionals.

3. *Ability to suspend judgment.* Helping professionals have heard it all! They can listen to "truth telling" from their clients and not be shocked. Most of the time, what clients need to be truthful about is not earth-shattering, except to them. Having a place to "release" frustration or anxiety and express their deepest desires or fear, as in the coaching relationship, is very freeing.

4. *Experience with confidentiality and ethics.* Professional therapists already respect confidentiality and have strong ethical guidelines. In fact, the boundaries and professional guidelines in therapy are so strong that new coaches will be surprised to find that coaching clients, who generally are not emotionally fragile, are looser with their own boundaries around privacy and confidentiality. Coaching clients are proud to have a coach and will not keep that a secret. However, the trained therapist-turned-coach will err on the side of strict confidentiality until clear guidance by the client redefines the expectations.

5. *Ability to seek solutions and think of possibilities.* Trained and experienced therapists are typically good solution seekers and possibility thinkers, and their professional training and experience have undoubtedly enhanced these skills. This is especially true for therapists who have embraced humanistic and client-centered paradigms, including the recent advances in positive psychology.

These are the five unique skills that experienced therapists bring to the coaching profession. Eventually, of course, the goal of masterful coaching is to digest the techniques, add new skills, and reach a level of comfort *being* a coach, which is more than just *doing* coaching!

## Adding Coaching as a Professional Service

If a therapist or counselor chooses to add life coaching to her practice, she can easily market her services nationally and even internationally with the practice of telephone coaching. Many therapists now offer therapy and counseling services via the Internet or telephone. Although we do not want to go into an extended discussion of teletherapy here, we do need to state that we believe it can be risky, depending on the client. Coaching should be done with mature, responsible persons. Therapy should be done *in person*, with occasional phone sessions when the person is not at risk or emotionally fragile. Adding coaching to your practice allows your business to grow geographically—you can live where you want without licensing concerns, and you can even travel and still be in contact with your coaching clients. The hourly fees also are higher than customary therapy fees, and clients may pay by a monthly "retainer," often for several months, if not years. Coaching clients stay for the long haul because they want to, not because they need to.

## Characteristics of Successful Coaches

As we mentioned earlier, life coaching is appealing to helping professionals who want to either add coaching to their business or move into coaching full-time (which can still include training, consulting, speaking, and writing). Most therapists are generally "people persons," meaning they like people, are pleasant, relate well with others, and want clients to have more fulfilling lives. But, as we all know, some therapists make us wonder how they stay in business—they either don't have effective professional personalities or good business sense, or both.

Through our anecdotal research and experience with the hundreds of therapists we have trained. we have found that those who are drawn to coaching tend to share important characteristics. You will notice that these characteristics also apply to well-adjusted, masterful therapists.

1. They are well-adjusted and constantly seek personal improvement or development.
2. They have a lightness of being and *joie de vivre*.
3. They are passionate about "growing" people.
4. They understand the distinction and balance between being and doing.
5. They are able to suspend judgment and stay open-minded.
6. They are risk takers who are willing to get out of their comfort zone.

7. They are entrepreneurial; even if they do not have great business skills, they are visionaries, able to see the big picture and reinvent themselves and their business to meet current trends.
8. They want to have a life and a business.
9. They have a worldview and tend to think more globally.
10. They are naturally motivational and optimistic.
11. They are great listeners and are able to empathize with their clients.
12. They are mentally healthy and resilient when life knocks them down.
13. Their focus is on developing the future, not fixing the past.
14. They are able to collaborate and partner with their clients, shedding the "expert" role.
15. They have a willingness to believe in the brilliance or potential for greatness in all people.
16. They look at possibilities instead of problems and causes (as do solution-focused therapists).
17. They exude confidence, and they are comfortable with not having all the answers.
18. They present as authentic and genuine, with a high degree of integrity.
19. They are willing to say, "I don't know" and explore where and how to learn what might be lacking.
20. They enjoy what they do and are enthusiastic and passionate about life.

As life coaching grows as a profession, many therapists with the above characteristics will recognize that they have been coaches for a long time—they just did not know what to call it! We strongly believe that the paradigm and the power of coaching will attract more healthy clients than therapy did. In fact, many of the "problems in living" for which clients sought the assistance of therapists are better served by a life coach—a relationship that avoids the stigma of therapy altogether.

Although new terminology may emerge in the future for the coaching relationship, the term *life coach (or personal coach)* fits well for now. Other terms, such as *personal consultant*, or *life strategist*, and so on, seem vague and constrained.

## Why Therapists as Coaches?

We believe that life coaching is part of a larger paradigm shift toward more people wanting to live their lives more purposefully. This shift might be considered a movement away from the paradigm of pathology to one of possibility. Many reasons for this shift could be cited, but they are beyond the scope of this book. At any rate, life coaching has evolved because it makes sense to people today to have a partner who elicits their unique greatness and who helps them move from mediocrity to excellence in living. Life coaching exists because it is helpful, and it prospers because it is transformational.

# CHAPTER TWO

# The History and Evolution
# of Life Coaching

*Change is the law of life, and those who look only to the past
or the present are certain to miss the future.*
—John F. Kennedy

Historical information provides current and prospective life coaches with both a framework for understanding their profession and insight into future opportunities. This framework also helps life coaches place themselves squarely within the larger context of a profession that is still changing and evolving. As we cast our eyes across the diverse threads of the past, perhaps we will come to understand the present more accurately and will be better prepared as life coaching expands in the 21st century. We believe an examination of the evolution of life coaching also helps therapists to make the transition to life coaching by further clarifying the similarities and differences between the two professions.

Systematic literature reviews and comprehensive historical accounts of the development of life coaching have not been conducted. We know of only one source, *The Handbook of Coaching* by Frederic Hudson (1999b), that includes historical content as part of the more extensive treatment of life coaching topics. No books on coaching have focused exclusively on the development of life coaching from its roots in modern psychology and counseling theories. This area is ripe for life coaching scholars interested in publishing opportunities.

The professional literature in business and human resource development refers to coaching as it developed in organizations (Hargrove, 1995; Whitmore, 1995), but documentation of the evolution of coaching, specifically life coaching, in the context of the helping professions is scant. Psychological theories (Freud, 1965; Hudson, 1999; Jung, 1953, 1976) of adult development, including psychosocial stage theories and the social theories of adult development, do offer opportunities for in-depth study for readers seeking a deeper theoretical perspective. Similarly, review of solution-focused therapy strategies and narrative therapy techniques (with which most therapists are already well acquainted) provides the reader with examples of psychotherapy techniques that develop the competence of the client. In fact, Bill O'Hanlon, who has authored more than a dozen books on solution-focused counseling approaches, suggested in a conversation with Pat that we not use the term *psychotherapy* and see it instead as "possibility counseling." And John Walter and Jane Peller (2000) boldly declared that psychotherapy should be called "personal consulting." That sounds like life coaching to us. These theorists and other modernists actually are stressing a nonpathological context for counseling. However, they are really referring to using coach-like skills with a therapy or counseling client. We want you to see that a life coaching relationship with a client is very distinct from just using coaching skills. It is a unique professional relationship in which a person explores with his or her coach (over time) how to live life more fully and *on purpose*.

The Resources section at the end of this book provides suggestions for future reading and exploration.

## The Evolution of Coaching Terminology

When we started our coaching careers, people would often ask, "What sport do you coach?" This is not surprising, given the history of the word coach and its tie to athletics. Now when we say "life coach," people still look at us curiously, but we no longer need to discuss "what sport." Our profession is receiving more and more public awareness and attention. And if they do ask, "What sport?" we answer, "The game of life!"

*Coaching* and *mentoring* have been common terms in the corporate environment for decades. Executive coaching has always been accepted as a perk or desirable form of consultation and support for high-level management. A distinction today, however, is mentoring, which is a service provided either formally or informally to train those employees who might be moving up the corporate ladder and so are mentored in the manager's ways. Corporate coaching today is provided both internally (by coaches who work for the company) and externally (by coaches hired by either the company or the managers themselves). Life coaching, however, has become desirable and accessible to those outside the corporate environment, and many corporate and business leaders do understand that, after all . . . it is ALL life coaching.

## The Psychological Roots of Life Coaching

Psychological theorists in the early part of the 20th century set the framework for life coaching's "whole and healthy person" view. The shift from seeing clients as ill or pathological toward viewing them as "well and whole" and seeking a richer life is paramount to understanding the evolution of life coaching. Life coaches view clients as whole and capable people and focus not on pathology, but on wellness.

Most people would agree that Sigmund Freud had a dramatic influence on society's view of mental illness. Although much of Freud's theory has little applicability to life coaching, he did profess that the driving influences in people's lives were not conscious (ego-driven) but unconscious forces—the id (libido) and the superego (social conscience)—which he believed were rich opportunities for analysis and dream interpretation. It is this emphasis on symbolic thinking that is beneficial for life coaching. Life coaches help clients discover their brilliance, which often lies masked or buried in their unconscious mind and can be accessed when they begin to design their lives consciously and purposely.

Colleagues from Freud's inner circle, such as Carl Jung and Alfred Adler, broke away from his theories of neuroses and psychosis, positing theories that were more teleological and optimistic about human potential. Although there remains a significant distinction between therapy approaches and coaching (which we discuss later in depth) many of Adler's and Jung's theories are antecedents to modern-day life coaching.

Adler, for example, saw himself as more of a personal educator, believing that every person develops a unique life approach that shapes his or her goals, values, habits, and personal drives. He believed that happiness arises from a sense of significance and social connectedness (belonging), not merely individual objectives and desires. Adler saw each person as the creator and artist of his or her life and frequently involved his clients in goal setting, life planning, and inventing their future—all tenets and approaches in life coaching today.

Similarly, Carl Jung believed in the power of connectedness and relationships, as well as a "future orientation" or teleological belief that we create our future through visioning and purposeful living. Jung's theories and approaches emphasized the transcendent values expressed as one goes though the process he called *individuation*—the progression and development of the self, the transcendent function. This process is particularly prevalent in the second half of life, a time when life coaches are most likely to experience this "life review" themselves and with their clients. Jung also described the importance of myths and rituals, which are becoming increasingly important components of our clients' lives. We believe therapist-trained coaches are particularly qualified to assist clients in these important stages of adult development.

## The Boulder Conference: Psychology Comes of Age

Clinical psychology, as a profession separate from research and academia, was catapulted into the latter half of the 20th century by the historical Boulder Conference in 1949—the first national meeting ever held in the United States to discuss standards of graduate training in psychology, despite the fact that doctoral programs in America had existed for more than 60 years (Albee, 2000). Up to that point, the emphasis was on theory and human behavior, not so much on clinical or psychotherapeutic applications in a systematized, integrated approach. After World War II the demand for psychologists and counselors grew in response to the need for treating post-traumatic stress (i.e., the psychological impact of war injuries) and the military's need to better prepare soldiers with an improved emphasis on mental health and the hope for a kind of "stress inoculation." Looking back now at the Boulder Conference, it is easy to see that the teaching of clinical psychology included much of what today is found in counseling psychology and even the offshoots of counseling and marriage and family therapy.

## Influences of Humanistic Psychology and the Human Potential Movement

During this time period, counseling and psychotherapy were starting to be viewed by many as arts more than sciences. The emergence of humanistic, client-centered approaches (Bugenthal, 1967; Fadiman & Frager, 1976; Frankl, 1959; Rogers, 1951; among others) framed the client as defined by potential and possibility, rather than neuroses or pathology.

In 1951, Carl Rogers's book *Client-Centered Therapy* defined counseling and therapy as relationships in which the client was assumed to have the ability to change and grow in the context of the clinician-created therapeutic alliance. This alliance evolved from a safe, confidential space granting the client or patient what Rogers called "unconditional positive regard." We believe this shift in perspective was a significant precursor to the development of life coaching.

In the years after World War II, American psychologists began to be influenced by European schools of thought, namely phenomenology and existentialism. These points of view laid much of the philosophical foundation for what was to become the Third Force* in psychological thought—humanistic psychology. (The early work of Carl Rogers, Kurt Lewin, Prescott Lecky and Abraham Maslow also served as important influences.) Emphasis is now focused on studying the whole person, not fragmented parts. Although the philosophies and values of humanistic psychology unified the whole field of psychology, they also polarized the profession. Humanistic psychology, which arose largely as a reaction against behaviorism's mechanistic view of humanity, was once again concerned with human experience and intrapsychic motivations, as it had been in psychology's earliest years, but these concerns were viewed as nonobservable, nonmeasurable, intervening variables in the precepts of behavioral psychology.

Abraham Maslow, considered by many to be the father of humanistic psychology, was largely responsible for injecting credibility and energy into the human potential movement of the 1960s, with the publication of his

---

*There are Four Forces: the First Force is Freudian psychology; the Second Force is behavioral psychology; the Third Force is humanistic psychology; and the Fourth Force is transpersonal psychology.

seminal treatise *Toward a Psychology of Being* (1962). In this work, Maslow summarized his research of "self-actualizing people" (a term first coined by Kurt Goldstein) and used terms such as "full-humanness," "being," and "becoming." This book is largely a continuation of theory he first posited in *Motivation and Personality* (1954, 1987). Maslow studied the "healthy personality" of people whom he termed self-actualizers; he researched, questioned, and observed people who were living with a sense of vitality and purpose, and who were constantly seeking to grow psychologically and achieve more of their human potential. It is this key point in history that we believe set the framework for the field of life coaching to emerge in the 1990s. Individuals seeking personal evolution and ways to live their life more fully do not need psychological counseling; life coaching is a more accurate paradigm for the improved outcomes or achievements these clients seek.

Maslow was instrumental in giving great value and importance to the idea of personal growth and its necessity for the healthy personality. However, Maslow was not the first to hold these ideas. Many early psychiatrists and psychologists revolted against the orthodox approaches to mental problems and their emphasis on the pathological or pathogenic components. The reader has already been introduced to the influential work of Adler and Jung, but Gordon Allport, James Bugental, Kurt Goldstein, Karen Horney, Sidney Jourard, Prescott Lecky, Rollo May, and Fritz Perls also influenced psychology's move toward a wellness perspective that laid much of the groundwork for modern coaching theory, perspective, and techniques.

Third Force psychology has found its place in mainstream psychology and is represented by an international organization. The first issue of the *Journal of Humanistic Psychology* was published in 1961 and edited by Anthony Sutich. The Association for Humanistic Psychology (AHP) began the following year. Abraham Maslow's ideas were central to the beginnings of both the journal and the association, but the AHP was not organized simply to promote his philosophy. The AHP represents a broad viewpoint, but it emerged as the Third Force (after Freudianism and behaviorism) in psychology because of its unitary revolt against mechanistic, deterministic psychology. We believe this philosophical shift took root in a generation that now rejects the idea of sickness and seeks wellness, wholeness, and purposeful living instead. Hence the emergence of life coaching!

## *Influences of Milton Erickson and Solution-Focused Approaches*

The work of Milton Erickson (the father of American hypnotherapy) is a key precursor to the methods used in coaching today. Erickson, an iconoclastic and unique psychiatrist, believed in the inherent ability of individuals to achieve wellness if the reason for an illness could be thwarted. He often achieved seemingly "miraculous results" from just a few sessions with a patient. Jay Haley (1986) coined the term "uncommon therapy" to describe Erickson's approach.

Bandler and Grindler (1975), who were students of Erickson, developed the approach called neuro-linguistic programming (NLP), which is an evolution of much Ericksonian theory and technique. This system focused on the powerful use of language and question-asking by the therapist to facilitate transformational change and achieve the client's desired outcome. Linguistics and inquiry are key aspects of the work of a life coach, and much of the heritage lies in the early work of Ericksonian practitioners. Erickson was noted for a "utilization approach," by which he made use of whatever the client brought (including the presenting symptom) as a treatment resource.

More recent psychological approaches that have evolved from Ericksonian and other wellness approaches are the solution-focused therapies. These approaches, which are not insight- or depth-oriented are also powerful influences on modern coaching practices and theory. In addition, Glasser's reality therapy, Ellis's rational emotive therapy, systemic family therapies (Haley, Madanes, Satir), psychosynthesis (Assagioli), and many hybrids of these lend themselves to coaching strategies. In all of these, the main focus is not pathology but behavior change through increased awareness and making choices that lead to desired future results and solutions to current "problems in living." For example, the work of Bill O'Hanlon (1999b) emphasizes possibilities and preferencing—an approach that fits well in life coaching relationships. The approaches of Steve de Shazer (1988) and his colleagues, called *solution-focused counseling*, could just as easily be called coaching. Many of their techniques and approaches for difficult clients have been adapted into coaching techniques, such as the miracle question and asking powerful questions that lead to action-oriented steps. In fact, Insoo Kim Berg and Peter Szabo wrote a book called *Brief Coaching for Lasting Solutions* since the first edition of this book.

Life coaching has, in essence, developed from three streams: (1) helping professions such as psychotherapy and counseling, and related theoretical perspectives as noted above; (2) consulting and organizational development, and industrial psychology; and (3) personal development trainings such as EST, Lifespring, Landmark Forum, and Anthony Robbins.

The personal development courses listed above all focus on taking personal action and responsibility for one's life choices. They often include one-to-one coaching as part of their service or recommend it to those who desire sustainable results from the weekend training experience.

## The Curse of the Medical Model

Unfortunately, somewhere along the way, the helping professions (spearheaded by clinical psychology) adopted, or were co-opted by, the medical model. The medical model sees the client as being ill and the patient with a diagnosis as in need of treatment or symptom relief. Although there clearly are some serious mental illnesses that benefit from clinical psychology or skillful psychotherapy, many people in the past were treated and labeled for what were really "problems in living"—situations or circumstances that did not need a diagnosis or assumption of pathology. Persons in the past seeking personal growth typically had nowhere to turn but to therapists, seminars, or self-help books. Sadly, many of these seminars and books also were problem-focused rather than looking forward for the powerful strategies of healthy life design.

Today, many clinicians find themselves on a dead-end street blocked by a corporate-managed health-care system where the main concern is financial profit, not mental health delivery. Unfortunately, most diagnoses pathologized people who weren't really mentally ill. These diagnoses became part of clients' permanent medical records, leading to embarrassment, insurance rejection, and other unnecessary problems. We believe society is ready for life coaching in which a relationship is sought to create a future—not to get over a past—and certainly not to receive a diagnosis for the effort.

Again, we believe psychotherapy and counseling can treat diagnosable mental illnesses and are effective (although the research on this point is disconcerting). However, these longer-term treatments (if you expect insurance to foot the bills) are often viewed as too expensive. Increasingly, the benefits of a relationship in which change and insight occur over time are not supported in the medical model. The counseling professions, in our opinion, fell into a trap after adopting the medical model and third-party payment for services. Now, in order to survive, counselors and therapists are reducing fees, and psychologists are even trying to obtain prescription privileges for psychotropic drugs, moving further into the medical arena. G. W. Albee (1998) says that psychologists (and other therapists) have "sold their souls to the Devil: the disease model of mental disorders" (pp. 247–248).

## Professional Associations and Growth of the Coaching Industry

As you have read, the influences of many psychological theorists and practitioners from the turn of the century to current times have contributed to the development and evolution of the field of life coaching.

Telecoaching—wherein coaches and clients talk by phone—was largely created and developed by an ingenious visionary named Thomas Leonard. In 1992 Leonard founded Coach University, which trains coaching students through classes taught be teleconference. At about the same time, Laura Whitworth, with the help of several colleagues, founded the Coaches Training Institute in San Francisco, which trains coaches through a series of weekend workshops and follow-up training by telephone. Leondard and Whitworth both worked for Werner Erhard, founder of EST training, and some of the early coach training was greatly influenced by the personal growth strategies of EST. In 1994 Whitworth and her colleagues also founded the Personal and Professional Coaches Association (PPCA), and in 1994 Thomas Leonard initiated the creation of the International Coach Federation (ICF), largely supported by Coach University. In 1996 the first annual ICF convention was held in Houston, Texas, with about 200 people in attendance. In 1997 the second annual ICF convention had over 300 in attendance, and Sandy Vilas (owner of Coach University) and Laura Whitworth (president of PPCA) announced the merger of the ICF and the PPCA into one body (The International Coach Federation).

Membership has grown exponentially since then. At the time of this printing, there are over 13,000 members of the ICF in more than 82 countries. Conferences are held regularly in the United States, Canada, Europe, Asia, and Australia. Several dozen coach training schools and universities have since developed coaching education programs using a combination of distance learning and in-person learning opportunities. Only a handful of these specialize in training mental health professionals to transition into coaching professionals. Since the emergence of the ICF in 1996, other organizations have also emerged to represent the coaching industry. The International Association of Coaching (IAC) was also founded by Thomas Leonard after he decided the ICF was not going in the direction he liked. The Worldwide Association of Coaching (WABC) represents qualified business coaches, and Coachville (*www.coachville.com*) became a resource center for coaching and developed more sophisticated training programs and annual conferences as its member-ship has grown. There are also many membership organizations in Europe and Australia that represent coaching, but the largest one worldwide is the ICF.

Patrick Williams started the Institute for Life Coach Training in 1998 and has trained thousands of clinicians and aligned professionals worldwide, with some of the curriculum translated into foreign languages.

## *Coach Training Opportunities*

Prior to the development of the coach training opportunities available today for this new profession, coaching was a term primarily used in the arts (voice coaches, drama coaches) and in the athletic and corporate worlds. Now, coaching is seen as both valuable and convenient to the general public for assistance in total life design. Due to the formal training available to prospective coaches who come from a variety of disciplines and work experiences, anyone can now find a personal coach who is well-trained to assist in achieving the big goals and desires of his or her personal and professional life. In addition to the growing number of accredited coach training programs by the ICF, dozens of graduate schools offer coaching certificates and graduate degrees (masters and doctorates) in coaching.

Life and business coaching began as a 20th-century phenomenon with roots in early psychological theories. It has blossomed in the 21st century worldwide. It is a profession still experiencing dynamic growth and change. Life coaching (and all its various specialties) will no doubt continue to interact developmentally with social, economic, and political processes, draw on the knowledge base of diverse disciplines, enhance its intellectual and professional maturity, and continue to establish itself internationally and domestically. Cooperative efforts among diverse professional groups will enable life coaching to develop in more unified and collaborative ways in order to strengthen its influence and serve a wider audience.

# CHAPTER THREE

# The Courage to Begin

*We gain a powerful perspective when we see courage as what we choose to do even when we feel afraid. Courage means accepting our feelings and sticking with our planned purposeful action.*

—Dave Ellis

From the day you realize you want more out of your life as a helping professional, every step you take to explore life coaching is a step closer to becoming the person you really want to be. We believe you can have what you want and that life coaching is a great way to get it. All you need is the courage to begin.

We have shared the stories of how we personally made this major life change and offered you insights into our transitions. There were times along the way when we analyzed our decisions and found ourselves fearful about making this change. Change always requires strength and determination; therefore, it is essential for you to be clear about your purpose and goals. Our search to renew our souls and our practices has been rewarded by the enhanced meaning we find in our work as healers and counselors. Additionally, we've discovered, to our great joy, that who we are now as life coaches is even better than who we were as therapists.

Similarly, this is the story of people like you whom we have met on our journey, such as therapists from workshops and conferences, people who call because they know someone we coached, faculty who have read our publications and are interested in the profession, and students in the Institute for Life Coach Training program. It is about helping professionals, just like you, who have laughed and cried and dreamed with us. This chapter tells the stories of their personal transition experiences in order to help you find the courage to begin to add coaching to your business or to make the gradual transition to a fulfilling business as professional coach.

## What Do You Want?

When we speak to groups of therapists who are interested in becoming coaches, they often reflect wistfully on their years working in a full, rewarding practice where their insurance payments flowed freely, their appointment books were full, and their communities held them in high regard as valued professionals. Nostalgia floats through the room and heads nod in agreement as these therapists speak.

My first five years out of graduate school were the best. I entered a group practice with three other therapists. It took awhile but, with their referrals, my practice started filling. Most of my clients had insurance and were delighted with my skills as a therapist. I really felt like I was making a difference.

One thing I loved about the "good ol' days" was my ability to work with the clients I really wanted to and the ones I felt I could help the most. It was challenging and stimulating. I looked forward to going to my office every day.

Back before we were the joke of TV sitcoms, there was a mystery to being a psychologist, and I kind of liked it that way. I felt as though the community respected us as professionals, and that felt good.

The wistfulness vanishes quickly when we ask therapists to describe the changes in their practice that cause them to consider life coaching as a career transition. The climate in the room shifts dramatically and body language alters.

I can't practice therapy—I'm too busy with the record-keeping the darn managed care organization requires of me. There isn't time to fill out the paperwork, let alone see the clients. A simple intake requires seven different forms and a call to the insurance company. Is this what I got my degree for?

Most days I find my successes with clients overwhelmed by the frustrations of doing HMO paperwork. I know I'm a good therapist, and I can make a difference, but it isn't fun any more.

Those therapists who have operated within the medical model frequently describe their practice as being increasingly buried under piles of paper generated by the managed care machine. No longer, they wail, does insurance support the therapy they believe their clients need or at least deserve.

I made seven calls and sent three sets of summary notes to the case review person before finally getting authorization to see this couple for two additional visits. By the time I called the couple back with the news, they were separated and one had left the state. I don't know—maybe it wouldn't have made a difference, but what it did do was take away my faith in this system of care.

Many describe having to choose between working under the shackles of a "bottom-line, profit hungry" insurance company and being pushed into trying to find enough clients who will pay out of pocket to sustain their floundering practices.

I know I need to expand my practice; I've got a daughter going to college next year. Over the past three years I've seen my third-party payment receipts decline dramatically. But there are only so many hours in the day. How am I ever going to meet the bills without working 50 or 60 hours a week?

Look, I'm a therapist, not a businessman. People say we need to be entrepreneurs and generate more clients who will pay our full fee, but I hate that stuff. I can't go to a Rotary Club and market myself like a car salesman. It's just not me.

Even those not caught up in the medical model describe feeling restless, wanting more, wanting to make a bigger difference.

I just feel as though there has to be more than what I'm doing now. I don't hate going to work, but it doesn't excite me very often any more. There has to be a better way to do this.

It is painful to observe the looks on the faces of new professionals just starting their careers. They describe wondering how they will ever be able to make a fruitful living as a therapist when those with far greater experience and training seem disillusioned and struggling.

I remember hearing some of my graduate faculty talking in hushed tones about the bleak market for new professionals. I didn't believe it was possible.

How am I ever going to make it? We want to get married when I finish my degree next summer, but I'm starting to worry about how much money I'll make as a therapist. I never really worried about it before, but when I hear people with far more experience than I have saying they aren't happy with their income streams and practices, I start to panic. Maybe I should have gone into computers.

Now, before you get too depressed, take a few moments and think about why you are considering a transition from therapy to life coaching. What about your current situation causes you to consider a change in how you operate as a helping professional? It is time to get personal. Make a list of five or more things you would like to change about your current situation.

Things that frustrate me about my current practice as a therapist are:

1.

2.

3.

4.

5.

Have more than five? Go ahead and add them to your list, but don't go on all day—there's a lot more to discuss!

The concerns we have recorded from therapists and the items you have probably listed are pervasive at every workshop we present and every time we discuss life coaching options individually with therapists. Typical concerns include:

1. Too many restrictions from insurance companies
2. Not enough clients
3. Not enough income
4. Lack of fulfillment
5. Don't know what to do to make it better

Therapists are usually very clear about what they don't like about their current situation and what they don't want to keep doing. It is easy to find a group of pessimistic therapists who are frustrated and exhausted. However, our experience is that many of the therapists in our workshops and our life coaching clients are challenged when faced with the change required to get what they do want. This is where you need to muster the courage to begin.

## The TRY IT! Exercises

In this book we present an assortment of ideas and exercises, and we ask that you try to do all of them. We have based these ideas and exercises on tools and techniques that have worked for our coaching clients and in our workshops. Just suspend your judgment and give them a try. If they work, great. If a particular one doesn't seem to fit, don't worry—a different one will. Again, our request is simple: Just try them!

Surprisingly, some people have a difficult time with this request. They want to analyze each exercise (this is especially true of therapists). If the idea conflicts with a way they have done things in the past, sometimes they just want to reject it. We ask you not to limit your ideas only to those you use now; otherwise you will finish this book in the same place you started. Also, if you limit your opportunity to try new things, you limit your potential to rediscover the creative energies inside you.

Dave Ellis, a professional colleague and friend of ours, has a great metaphor for what we are talking about. His super book, *Becoming a Master Student* (1999), presents many fantastic tools and strategies to help students succeed in college. One concept that fits perfectly for life coaching is that "ideas are tools." For example, when you use a new hammer, you might notice its shape, weight, and balance, but you do not analyze the hammer or try to figure out if the hammer is right for you—you just use it. If it works, you will use it again. If it doesn't work, you find a new hammer. You do not have to like or even agree with the hammer as the tool of choice. Just suspend judgment and TRY IT!

This is what we are asking you to do throughout this book. When we present a new idea or want you to take on an assignment we believe will foster success, we will precede the task with this header—TRY IT! Are you ready to try some new tools to help you become a great life coach?

---

## ☞ TRY IT! ☜

Since you are reading this instead of being on the phone with us once a week as our coaching client, we want to make sure you have a record of your progress through this experience. (Yes, we are confident you *will* make progress.) Therefore, we want you to get a journal so you can record your thoughts and ideas, as well as set some goals for your life coaching career.

Treat yourself to a journal that feels like you. Take a special shopping trip to find one with the right design, texture, color, shape, and paper. Do you want lined or unlined paper? Do you want a pocket-size journal or a larger one? A good journal gives you plenty of room to write and can be carried easily so you can capture those great ideas that come up during the day. Some people prefer to use a software journaling program such as the one found at *www.lifejournal.com*. If that works best for you, go for it, but you'll want a way to record your thoughts *as you are on the go*. Your journal should be sacred and always available for your thoughts,

*continued on next page*

---

ideas, insights, frustrations, and victories. Rereading your entries over time will accelerate your evolution as a coach and the growth of your business possibilities and opportunities. The key point is to find what feels right for you and is functional so that you use it!

We have a pretty clear picture of what you don't want in your career. You listed these points earlier, and we shared comments from some of our participants and clients. Be sure to write these in your journal. Shifting from what isn't working to a new, more functional and fitting model is not an alien concept, but, surprisingly, therapists often fail to apply it to themselves. When we ask therapists to tell us what they *do* want in their careers, the responses are interesting.

Hmmmm . . . gee, I don't know. I guess I want more money, less work, more prestige, and a lot more fun.

I want more time to enjoy my life. I want exercise and balance and time to write. I want to enjoy my children and be home when they get home from school.

I want to be true to my values in working with my clients. I feel managed care has forced me into a bind between doing what I believe is right for my clients and doing what they will pay for. I'm doubting my abilities and myself. I want to feel strong, positive, and capable as a helper.

It seems I'm clearer about what I don't want than what I do want. There has to be something more than this—a better way of doing the helping work that is challenging, fun, makes a difference, and also gives me energy rather than drains me on a daily basis.

## ☞ TRY IT! ☜

What do I want for my business? This is a very important question for your transition journey. What do you want? Really want? Really, really, really want? Deb often leads coaching workshop participants through a focused visualization exercise in which they identify and list some of their wants in major categories of their lives.

Find a quiet place where you can have uninterrupted time to think about your life. What do you *have* in your life that you want more of? What *don't* you have that you'd like added to your life? What do you *have* or *do* that you'd like to change or eliminate? What have you dreamed about or always wanted to *do* but just haven't taken steps toward achieving, for whatever reason? Think about the person you are and what you really value in your life. What would you do to *be* different in your life?

In your journal, write what you want in answer to the questions below. Deb has offered a list of wants from herself and clients as examples to help you see how we write them. The more specific you are, the more likely you are to get what you really want.

Here are some examples of written wants from Deb and some of her clients. Notice the pattern of the "want statements."

I want daily reflection and journaling time in my schedule.

I want a simplified record-keeping process for my finances.

I want to only take on work that feels like play.

I want to travel with my husband for a month in New Zealand.

I want my children and grandchildren to have the lives of their dreams.

I want to eat only nutritious foods and to exercise on a daily basis.

I want to develop deep, soulful relationships with special people in my life.

I want to retire at 50.

I want to spend more time with my family.

I want to get a massage.

*continued on next page*

I want to wear only clothes that feel like pajamas.
I want to celebrate daily my wonderful life and many blessings.

The great thing about wants is that they are freely exchanged. If you see a want on the above list that applies to you, write it on your list. In workshops we freely exchange wants, which helps all of us think more creatively.

So, following the above pattern of *I want* _____, answer the following questions for yourself. Write your want statements in your journal, one per line. Write whatever (*having*, *doing*, or *being*) comes up after reading the question—as many wants as you can think of.

In the life area of *relationships*, what do you want?
In the life area of *leisure*, what do you want?
When you think about your *finances*, what do you want?
What to you want in the area of *health* and *wellness*?
When you think about what you want for your *family members*, what do you discover?
What do you want in the life area of your *work* or your *career*?
What do you want in the life area of *spirituality*?
When you think about *making a difference in your world* or *being of service*, what do you want?
When you think about the area of *travel*, what do you want?
Want do you want in the area of your *continuing education*?
What have you been dreaming about that you *really, really, really want*?

Spend some time recording your wants. After writing all you can, come up with two to three really significant wants in each life area that you'd like to work on achieving. Contemplate these wants as you continue your journey. Write them each on a 3 × 5 card and place them someplace so that you will see them every day—such as on your bathroom mirror, your car steering wheel, your computer monitor or your cell phone. If the wants are truly important, you will use them to guide your actions as you develop your life coaching practice. Make a plan today to start getting what you want in your life.

## Do You Have What It Takes?

We have already told you we believe that therapists are eminently qualified to be life coaches. You are well educated and well trained, you possess the necessary critical helping skills, and you have many other skills and talents. All of these are essential ingredients for successful life coaches. If we asked you to write your qualifications in your journal, you could come up with a long list. Other than additional training specific to life coaching, you are ready to start today. So, what is holding you back?

During our experience coaching and training hundreds of therapists over the course of the last several years, we have discovered what we believe to be the most important ingredient for a successful transition from therapist to life coach. It isn't where you went to college or how you were trained as a therapist. It isn't how successful your therapy practice has been or even how many years you have been a helping professional. The most important indicator of success in transitioning from therapist to life coach is your ability to make a change. Plain and simple.

We have seen relatively new therapists transition smoothly into a full-time life coaching practice in a short time, whereas experienced professionals struggled to infuse coaching into their practices on even a part-time basis. This journey will require you to think and act differently as a helping professional. We'll discuss some of these differences more specifically later. We understand it is scary to let go of the way you have always worked and try something new. This is plain old fear, a common emotion for individuals facing any transition. Whether you are planning to close your therapy practice completely and jump headfirst into life coaching or whether you want to stick your toes in first and try it on a part-time basis, some fear is often associated.

As we tell our therapy clients, these fears are likely based on our negative beliefs about the world or ourselves. If you hold on to these fears, you won't be able to take the risks, seize the opportunities, and develop the positive perspective necessary to function successfully as a life coach. Many therapists share a fear of marketing themselves as a life coach, of managing their coaching practice as a business. You may share this fear or have other fears that occur to you as you read this chapter. You can recognize them as the little voice in the back of your head trying to persuade you to put this book down and go back to doing what you know how to do—therapy. Stay with these thoughts and feelings a little longer, and record them in your journal.

---

## ☞ TRY IT! ☜

As you try to see yourself developing a new practice as a life coach, what negative beliefs or fears stand in your way? Make a list of these in your journal. Put an asterisk by the ones that seem most powerful. Here are a few we have gathered from our clients and ourselves:

I'll go broke!
I can't market myself!
I can't run a business!
No one is going to pay me to do this!
I'm throwing away an expensive education and a lot of training!

It has been our experience that, in time, as you learn more about life coaching and have some successes, the fears subside and you are ready to go for what you really want. Find support, try new things, and see yourself in a new light. All we ask is for you to be a willing, active, and involved participant.

---

## ☞ TRY IT! ☜

Write your life story in your journal. How did you come to this point in your personal and professional world? Give yourself at least an hour for this exercise.

## Total Life Design

If you are going to be a credible coach, live your life as you coach others to live theirs. This does not mean your life has to be perfect. Living purposefully means living in full awareness of what can be improved in your life and what you want to maintain or eliminate. This is why we believe it is essential that you also have a personal coach, especially in the beginning of your transition. Even later, when you are successful, having your own coach keeps you focused on what really matters and aware of how your clients may experience the process of coaching. We both have had coaches throughout our transitions and have hired specialists from time to time.

Much of our approach is presented as Total Life Coaching™. We coach from a client-centered, whole-person approach, with the knowledge and experience that coaching for improvement in one area of a clients life will undoubtedly affect many other areas. They are all connected.

Once again, here is our definition of life coaching:

Life coaching is a powerful human relationship where trained coaches assist people to design their future rather than get over their past. Through a typically long-term relationship, coaches aid clients in creating visions and goals for ALL aspects of their lives and creating multiple strategies to support achieving those goals. Coaches recognize the brilliance of each client and their personal power to discover their own solutions when provided with support, accountability and unconditional positive regard

Since the first edition of this book was published, Pat has co-written his second book, *Total Life Coaching: 50+ Life Lessons, Skills, and Techniques to Enhance Your Practice and Your Life*. We believe that Total Life Coaching is the operating system for all coaching, whether it is business, executive, corporate, or personal coaching. As the operating system, it is always in the background of all coaching conversations. For example, a client may be focused on career-specific changes, but as a coach you can also bring up ways to at least look at other areas of his or her life that may benefit from some attention. We use a Life Balance Wheel or coaching mandala (included in the Welcome Packet at the back of this book) as a system for exploring clients' main life areas and helping them learn that a balanced life most often leads to successful manifestation of their goals in any one area of their life. Later, you will have an opportunity to work with the coaching mandala.

## Living Your Life on Purpose

Truly effective coaching unleashes the spirit and deep desires, expands the client's capacity to achieve real change, and can even catalyze personal transformation. This degree of change does not occur with simple techniques such as goal setting and motivation. It occurs when coaching considers the underlying context for change and alters the client's experience of living more *on purpose*. If you are going to be an effective coach in a whole-person context, we believe it is essential for you to have done the work yourself. Most coach training programs teach a variety of techniques and strategies for coaching, but many are about external skills. To be a truly masterful coach, you also must work on changing from within because the profession of coaching is more about your *beingness* than about skills or techniques.

Many of us have experienced psychotherapy as clients perhaps as an educational requirement or because we had our own healing work to do. Similarly we believe that masterful coaches must experience coaching on a regular basis and work with a coach on the very issues or desires from which their clients will also benefit. For us, that starts with looking at one's life purpose or life design.

Clients indeed come to coaching for more mundane reasons than designing their life, but whatever the presenting objectives, there is always the possibility of introducing the concept of Total Life Coaching. For that process, you as the coach must have experienced the power of designing your life and living more purposefully. You will have an opportunity to explore your life purpose in a future exercise.

Some coaching schools call this concept "coaching from the inside out." We consider it part of a coach's total life design, but whatever you call it, we believe that it will help you discover ways to coach your clients about life design and personal fulfillment. In the process, this concept will be useful and perhaps even transformational for you as well. Being able to "walk the talk" as a coach means that you have experienced what you suggest for your clients and that you implement the skills so that your life is a model for your clients. Again, this does not mean that you are living the life of a saint or that you are an enlightened master; it means that you live your life purposefully and are aware when you get in your own way. You must be committed to modeling the experience of living a fulfilling life or of being *on the path* to creating a fulfilling life. You generally will attract clients who are one step behind or one step ahead of where you are. Remember, sometimes the student is also the teacher.

## Coaching as an Interdevelopmental Process

As you work on living your life more authentically, you will also come to find that much of the joyfulness of the coaching profession is that both you and the client evolve. For you to model a great life, you should be living a great life or at least moving rapidly on that path. Your life cannot be a mess if your coaching business is going to thrive or if your coaching is to be truly effective. Your personal transformation provides practical magic for your clients.

---

### ☞ TRY IT! ☜

Using the Life Balance Wheel (Figure 3.1), give yourself a score from 1 to 10 in each of the life areas. Which ones show the biggest gap between where you are now and where you want to be? Identify and record in your journal what you want to do to make the scores higher (to at least an 8). Now, who can help you work on closing these gaps? Do you have a coach or a buddy, or can you work on these gaps yourself? We recommend that you work with your own coach, because this is exactly where you will also start with your clients. Write in your journal what you discovered during this exercise, and identify three actions you will take in the next week to help you narrow the gaps and achieve what you want.

---

**Figure 3.1.** Life Balance Wheel (Coaching Mandala)

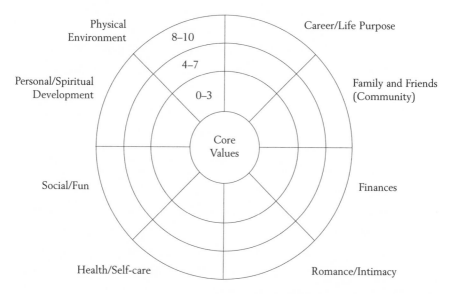

Physical Environment
8–10
4–7
0–3
Core Values
Career/Life Purpose
Personal/Spiritual Development
Family and Friends (Community)
Social/Fun
Finances
Health/Self-care
Romance/Intimacy

© Patrick Williams, Institute for Life Coach Training

The hub represents your core values—each area interrelated in an ideal life. Give yourself a score (1–10) and shade or color in the space accordingly. Use this coaching mandala as a way to assess the level of life satisfaction in each area. You may score it numerically to measure the improvement desired, or you may use it to have a coaching conversation about gaps between where you are now and where you would like to be.

We are going to provide a taste of the total life coaching concept. The purpose of this chapter is not to give you all the methods for this total life-design work, which are available in our formal coach training program through the Institute for Life Coach Training. However, we will give you the key starting point for your journey into coaching.

## De-cluttering Your Life

After completing your Life Balance Wheel assessment, the next step is to look at what gets in your way of having a great life. We call this process "de-cluttering" because it invariably involves the actual tossing out and cleaning up of clutter—piles of papers, old magazine clippings, clothes that no longer fit, broken kitchen appliances, and all the stuff we save for years because we think we might need it someday—all the stuff that clutters our closets, our garages, our offices, and our lives. Believe us when we say that getting rid of physical clutter actually helps you gain energy in your life. A part of you is connected to all your stuff, and the more organized and uncluttered your physical space is, the more room you have for what you really want.

This is equally true for the nonphysical clutter in your life—emotional baggage that still needs unpacking, important conversations that needed attending to in significant relationships, and handling concerns about money, your body, and so on. These are not necessarily therapy issues. They are just psychological clutter that needs to be handled. This is a great area to work on with a mentor coach.

### Energy Drainers and Energy Gainers

Cheryl Richardson speaks of eliminating things that drain you and replacing them with things that fuel you in her book *Take Time for Your Life* (1998). This is common terminology and practice in the coaching field. Energy drainers are those things (activities, habits, relationships, or clutter) that cost you energy. These are the items on your to-do list, procrastinations, piles of files, or anything else that you have not finished doing or dealing with. As each item is handled, you reclaim the energy that was attached to it. Then you have more energy to focus on what really matters. You can have more choice in your life. In fact, we believe that depression is actually depletion and that as people replenish themselves by eliminating energy drainers and choosing more energy gainers, they will be less depleted (and less depressed). Our friend and fellow coach Philip Humbert calls this work "personal ecology."

## ☞ TRY IT! ☜

### The First Steps of De-cluttering

Using the forms below, make a list of what you are putting up with at work and at home to determine what energy drainers might be limiting you right now. Now is the time to identify those things. As you think of more items, add them to your list. You may or may not choose to do anything about them right now, but just becoming aware of and articulating them will bring them to the forefront of your mind, where you'll naturally start eliminating, fixing, or resolving them.

For example, look at your office. Your office is the seat of your coaching business. Creating space in your office is the first step toward creating space in your life for your coaching business. Is there clutter? Disorganization? Is it set up in such a way as to give you energy? Does your office make you feel peaceful and comfortable? Make your workspace perfect for you, even if you work at home. You must have the physical space, the time space, and the emotional space for you to transition to *being* a coach.

Other places to look for energy drainers are in relationships that have what Fritz Perls (1973) called "unfinished business." You might need to have what we call a "courageous conversation" to clean up some part of the relationship. You will regain energy when you do. You can also look at your to-do list and other things you have wanted to work on. Make it a priority to take care of all the things on this list by focusing and committing. Coaching wisdom includes this edict: Do it, dump it, or delegate it. Look at the tasks at hand and the things you are putting up with, follow that wisdom, and complete anything that needs your attention.

| ENERGY DRAINERS AT WORK | ENERGY DRAINERS AT HOME |
| --- | --- |
| 1. | 1. |
| 2. | 2. |
| 3. | 3. |
| 4. | 4. |

*continued on next page*

| ENERGY DRAINERS AT WORK | ENERGY DRAINERS AT HOME |
|---|---|
| 5. | 5. |
| 6. | 6. |
| 7. | 7. |
| 8. | 8. |
| 9. | 9. |
| 10. | 10. |

Now, after you have experienced great relief in whittling down your list of energy drainers, it is important to go the extra step and choose consciously to have energy *gainers* in your life. These may fall in the realm of positive daily or weekly habits, such as exercise, meditation, or time with friends, family, and your spouse or life partner. Energy gainers are those things or activities that give you a charge of joy, fun, and passion, or peace and comfort. We often have these in our life, but they get pushed aside by the energy drainers. As you take care of your energy drainers, you now have time to choose energy gainers purposefully.

## The Second Step of De-cluttering
*(Charging the Batteries)*

Make a list of those things that impact your life in a positive way. They can be things you do (or want to do more of), people you like to be around, or favorite aspects of your physical environment (artwork, music, an organized living or work space).

One of our clients gets energy in her work environment from having a stereo in her office and a supply of soothing CDs; another gets energy from a daily jog with colleagues in her work area; another loves to help coordinate a biweekly potluck for her office staff. At home, one client engages in a daily journaling ritual in a special place with fragrant candles; another schedules a weekly lunch out with a friend where they

*continued on next page*

always have a healthy and nutritious meal; a third schedules a massage in his hotel room when he is traveling away from home. Make a list of some energy gainers you'd like to bring into your life.

| ENERGY GAINERS AT WORK | ENERGY GAINERS AT HOME |
|---|---|
| 1. | 1. |
| 2. | 2. |
| 3. | 3. |
| 4. | 4. |
| 5. | 5. |
| 6. | 6. |
| 7. | 7. |
| 8. | 8. |
| 9. | 9. |
| 10. | 10. |

## Strengthening Your Personal Integrity

A big part of your work as a coach is to live with a high degree of personal integrity. What do we mean? In engineering, *integrity* refers to the solidness in the foundation of the structure. The integrity of a bridge or skyscraper depends on a strong foundation and structure that ensure the safety and functionality of the final creation. We are no different. For the design, creation, and structure of our lives to be the best they can be, we must have a strong personal integrity or foundational congruence. In other words, we are out of integrity if our underlying foundation is weak and we are not able to stand tall and firm in the life we want to live.

Having integrity as a coach means doing what it takes to make your vision of a fulfilling, purposeful life a reality. Much of the work here involves aligning your values with your purpose and vision for your ideal life, and then finding ways to turn them into reality rather than wishes. Much of this work is part of a good coach training program that emphasizes the importance of personal transformation work for successful life coaching. It is beyond the scope of this book to present this detailed training, but we will reference training and reading throughout our book that we believe will further enhance your personal integrity. This is another perfect opportunity to work with a mentor coach.

## Finding Yourself and Renewing Your Soul

We believe that we are even better helping professionals as life coaches than we were as therapists. Time and again we hear the same response from therapists who have made the transition. Here's what Carole Kunkle-Miller, one of our graduates and a former full-time therapist, has to share:

> I was skeptical as to whether I could really make the transition from full-time psychologist to coach. I moved slowly at first, probably due to my fears about giving up the known to face the unknown. I have now learned to think about myself and my gifts in a big way, much different than I had ever thought of myself before. I now have a popular e-zine, an interview with *Working Woman* magazine, and an interview with National Public Radio, and my coaching clients are quickly growing. Managed care is not totally out of my picture yet, but imagine my excitement to write a letter of resignation to one of the big companies this week. I don't need them anymore. What a wonderful transformation!!!

You are not alone on this journey. We will help coach you through this transition as you participate in activities and explorations. We will provide rich resources carefully designed to help you find yourself and renew your soul as a helping professional. You will also be joined in spirit by the words of two therapists (Pat and Deb) who have joyfully made the transition, and you will also learn from participants in the Institute for Life Coach Training program. As you begin to realize that it is the quality of your efforts that matters, failure becomes unthinkable. How can you fail to become yourself? Are you ready to begin? Do you have what it takes to learn new skills, unlearn old ones, and be persistent?

# ≺ PART II ≻
# Life Coaching for Therapists

# CHAPTER FOUR

# Therapy and Coaching:
## *Distinctions and Similarities*

*If you want to change attitudes, start with a change in behavior.*
—William Glasser

The ability to change is a premier prerequisite for making a successful transition from mental health counseling (or related profession) into life coaching, and we recognize that change takes courage. We hope that you are excited about the opportunities life coaching offers for both helping professionals and clients, and that you are ready to proceed with learning more of the nitty-gritty details.

Beyond the ability to change, our research indicates two additional attributes you'll want to develop to have a successful coaching practice:

1. An understanding of the distinctions between therapy and coaching.
2. The business and entrepreneurial skills necessary to build a successful coaching practice.

We discuss business and entrepreneurial skills later in the book. For now, let's examine distinctions, and then similarities, between coaching and therapy.

## Distinctions between Therapy and Coaching
As the profession of life coaching evolves, it becomes more uniquely defined and described. Over the past several years we've seen increasing clarity about the role and distinctions within coaching (Williams, 2004a, 2004b). These

distinctions continue to emerge even as you read this book. Increasingly, we believe that life coaching is an evolutionary step beyond traditional therapy. We don't believe traditional therapy will become extinct, but, we do believe that it will be associated more with the clients who need clinical services. On a continuum, it might look something like this:

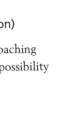

| **Traditional Therapy—** (old style) | **Transitional Models—** (gray areas) | **Coaching—** (a new option) |
|---|---|---|
| Psychoanalytic | Solution-focused, brief | Whole-life coaching |
| Paradigm of pathology | Paradigm of solutions | Paradigm of possibility |
| Orientation | | Orientation |
|    Process | |    Outcome |
|    Feelings | |    Action |
|    Inner world | |    Inner to outer worlds |
| History | Language is primary | Vision of Future |
| "Why?" |    tool | "How?" |
| Therapist is expert | Move away from | Coach as cocreator |
| Client is patient |    pathology | Partnership of equals |
| Medical model | | Freedom from managed care |

Just as some of the traditional models blended into more solution-focused perspectives and clients moved between the two, we believe cross-referrals will occur between solution-focused therapists and coaches as the public becomes clearer about the appropriateness of each profession. Several leaders in the solution-focused movement, including Insoo Kim Berg (1994, 2005) and Steve de Shazer (1985), have used powerful language and possibility-oriented strategies, which are very useful for therapists transitioning into life coaching. The distinctions between the solution-focused therapies and coaching are not as simple to delineate, because they blend more than coaching does with traditional, more analytical models of therapy. Again, we believe that as the helping professions continue to evolve, clients will be able to more clearly determine who is the "best fit" for their current concern. Figure 4.1 illustrates our thinking.

**Figure 4.1** Therapy and Coaching in Relationship

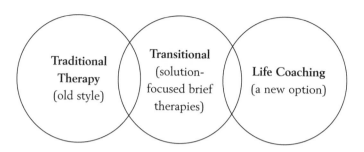

We consider the distinctions between traditional therapy and coaching in terms of four broad categories.

1. Perspectives on the process: *past vs. future*. Therapy focuses on the past and generally assumes that the client has a problem that needs solving; coaching focuses on the future and assumes that the client is whole and capable of having a wonderful life.
2. Why clients come to see you: *fix vs. create*. Clients seek a therapist as a source of fixing or eliminating their problem; clients seek a coach to help them get more out of their lives or to create new possibilities in their lives.
3. Characteristics of the helper–client relationship: *professional vs. collegial*. Therapy clients see the therapist as an expert who holds the answers and techniques to fix their problems; coaching clients see the coach as a partner to support their growth and efforts to create an even better life than they have now.
4. How you generate new clients: *limited vs. open*. Therapists are limited in the ways they can generate clients and how readily they can approach others about their services; coaches can be free and open about seeking clients and discussing their services.

We consider each of these distinction categories individually and then move on to how therapy and coaching are similar.

## Perspectives on the Process: Past versus Future

From our perspective, therapy has historically addressed the client's past and some form of pain or dysfunction. The helper's role was to bring the client to an adequate or reasonable level of current functioning (taking the dysfunction into consideration). Coaching, by contrast, works with an individual who already is adequately functioning and moves with him to a higher level of functioning.* Imagine you are driving your car down the freeway. If you look in the rearview mirror toward where you have been, you look at the past—that is therapy. If you look out the front windshield toward where you are going and the road beyond your vision, you look toward the future—that is life coaching.

Now, we know some of you reading this are saying, "But I work in the future when I do therapy!" This may well be the case, particularly if you are trained in and practice from a solution-focused perspective. However, we would suggest that if you are helping adequately functioning individuals move to higher levels of functioning by using coaching techniques, you probably aren't doing therapy—or at least therapy as defined by most insurance companies. We recognize there are some coach-like therapists. In fact, they are usually the individuals most comfortable with the therapist-to-coach transition.

Traditional psychotherapy focuses on the root of the problem, the history, the family of origin, the everything of origin! Coaching, from a theoretical perspective, focuses on the future, barrier identification, goal setting, planning, and creative action. Coaching works actively with the conscious mind in order to help the client step into a preferred future while also living a fulfilling life in the present.

## Why Clients Come to See You: Fix versus Create

In most clinical practices, clients arrive with a presenting problem that they want you to solve or because someone has sent them to see you so you will "fix" them. We see a lot of the latter in marital therapy.

---

*While it is not the focus of this book, we'd like to note that there are coaches who have specialties working with people who might not fall into the category of "adequately functioning." For example, there are specialized coaches who work within a school system with disturbed youth who are also in therapy.

# Therapy and Coaching

If you applied the traditional medical model of therapy, you'd undertake strategies similar to the following: First, you would talk with the client about her personal and medical histories, as well as previous mental health treatment. You would explore the history and duration of the problem. You would talk about why she believes she might have this problem at this time in her life and continue to gather pertinent current and historical information. Next, you would get out your DSM (*Diagnostic and Statistical Manual*) and, based on all the history and information you have gathered, you would give the client a diagnosis and develop a treatment plan.

Now, if the client has insurance, the diagnosis is hopefully one that the insurance company will accept. If not, you face the common dilemma of deciding whether you will assign a DSM diagnosis that would enable the client to get insurance reimbursement. Many therapists face this decision on a daily basis and often will assign a DSM diagnosis simply to enable the client to get reimbursement, not because the diagnosis is helpful in any way. This is the sad reality of managed care and the medical model in the helping professions.

Beyond the above dilemma, we must consider the client's perspective throughout this relationship. Clients assume that they will be "fixed"—that they will experience emotional healing—as a result of their relationship with a therapist because that is why they wanted therapy in the first place.

A coaching client, on the other hand, comes to see you for a myriad of reasons, but most of them relate to her future. She's probably heard of you from a friend or colleague who also has a life coach and is doing great things with his or her life. She usually does not come because she has a major problem, certainly not a major psychological one. She is not coming with a dysfunction. Typically she is not coming in pain. She might have a little general malaise because she is wanting *more* out of her life and doesn't know how to get it. She doesn't need, or usually even desire, a diagnostic label. She doesn't have something broken that she needs an expert to "fix." She just wants something more out of work, relationships, career, spiritual practice, or physical wellness, to name a few opportunities. The assumption is that by working with you, she will have greater success in planning, setting goals, and creating the life of her dreams. Coaching is not about fixing—coaching is about *creating*.

If a client with a major psychological problem seeks out your coaching services, the appropriate action is to refer that client to a qualified therapist. Our coach training program curriculum speaks to this area in depth and further addresses the nuances for professionals who want to maintain both a therapy and a coaching practice. As a general rule of practice, we believe that you should keep miles between your coaching and therapy practices if you choose to have both. Additionally, we believe that once a person has been your coaching client, you should not take him or her into your therapy practice. The reverse is mostly true, but a therapist may do coaching with a former therapy client as long as there is a ritual ending of the therapy relationship, and the new coaching relationship is begun formally and clearly. Most of our graduates leave counseling or an aligned profession for a complete transition into coaching and maintain a list of qualified therapists for referrals. Others do both counseling and coaching, but not with the same client. Likewise, we know therapists who refer clients to life coaches when the clients have resolved their therapeutic issues and are ready to move forward with their life design and plans.

## Characteristics of the Helper–Client Relationship: Professional versus Collegial

In the therapeutic relationship, the therapist is often assumed to be the "expert," and sometimes therapists feel that clients expect them to know the solution to their problems. The power, at least from the client's view, typically rests with the therapist. This is one of the reasons why we spend so much time in our therapeutic training learning about boundaries, ethical standards, transference, and all the other issues revolving around the counselor–patient relationship. We understand that some of you do all you can to ensure that your clients keep their power in your therapeutic practice; however, you must admit that when you get down to the nitty-gritty, you, the therapist, are guiding the counseling process. As the professional, you hold a great deal of power in the relationship, whether you want it or not.

## *Active Partnership*

In contrast, the coaching relationship is egalitarian, more like an active partnership. A successful life coaching relationship is collegial and balanced. Life coaches recognize that clients really have the knowledge and the solutions; coaches simply help unlock their brilliance. Consider this dialogue difference between therapy and coaching clients.

> THERAPY CLIENT: "I just don't know what is the matter with me—I'm so depressed."
>
> COACHING CLIENT: "I'm not sure where to go next; I want to have more time with my family, but I'm just not sure how to make it work and keep this job."

Coaching clients often know where they want to go; coaches help them clarify goals so they can see their way more clearly. There is no power differential, per se, in coaching. Good coaches make a conscious effort to keep the relationship balanced. Again, we recognize that some of you conduct your therapeutic sessions more like the life coaching sessions we described than traditional therapy sessions. That's great—you are that much closer to practicing successfully as a life coach!

If you were to observe a coaching session, you would see that it is typically very open, often friendly, casual, and light. Life coaches laugh with their clients and, when appropriate, may even joke or gently tease. With caution, life coaches may feel comfortable sharing personal experiences that are pertinent to what the client is experiencing. Clients and coaches feel as though they know each other on a deeper level than is possible in many other professional relationships. Coaching clients frequently report that they appreciate that openness.

We want to be very clear here that we believe coaches are professionals and should act accordingly. We endorse the ICF Code of Ethics (see Resources) and train from a model that endorses high standards of professional behavior. The difference we are addressing is the relationship between the coach and the client, and how each perceives the other and their relationship.

## Public Contact

Another difference between coaching and therapeutic relationships is how you handle public contact with your client. Yes, you do maintain confidentiality, and, unless your client gives permission, you do not automatically disclose that she is a client. This issue is something you discuss up front with the client during the intake interview and that we discuss further in chapter seven. Most coaching clients readily offer permission for disclosure, and the level of openness is far greater than typically permitted in a therapeutic relationship. You can even talk to a client in the grocery store. Here is Deb's story:

> When I was practicing in a small town in rural south central Alaska, I always felt awkward seeing my therapy clients at the mall or grocery store because I was so conscious of confidentiality concerns. In no way did I want to violate their right to privacy or let on that they were seeing me to others who clearly knew my work. It was always a dance as to whether to acknowledge them or not, and when I didn't, I felt uncomfortable even though we'd discussed confidentiality in therapy and how that translated to the real world.
>
> Sometimes they'd say, "Hi, Dr. Deb" and my young daughter would say, "How do you know them?" and I'd say, "Uh . . . from work" . . . and she'd say, "Oh, I get it." Now, as a coach, when I meet a client we often hug and share warm greetings. Frequently, clients introduce me to friends or family members by saying, "Hey, here's Deb—she's my coach." Typically the friend responds with, "Yeah? What sport?" and we are off on the path of defining and clarifying life coaching.

Coaching clients appreciate not having the stigma attached to life coaching that unfortunately can still accompany therapy. Although society is changing, coaching clients are much more likely to tell others that they are seeing or talking to a life coach than they would be disclosing that they work with a therapist.

### How, When, and Where We Meet Clients

Life coaching can occur in a variety of formats. The options are numerous with regard to location and time frames. You might meet your client in a coffeehouse, your office, an airport club lounge, or exclusively on the telephone. Likewise, you could meet for half an hour, an hour, or a full day. Many coaches meet with their clients for 1- to 2-day sessions, usually once a year or perhaps in the beginning of the relationship. Due to the time and cost, this option is usually for the executive or business owner. During these intensive coaching sessions, the coach usually explores all life areas in more depth with the client and they cocreate detailed action plans and identify ways to address obstacles. They may develop a clearer vision and mission, both professional and personal, and create a Total Life Plan, designing the focus and intentions for many months or even years ahead. These "intensives" are a powerful way to create a strong relationship between coach and client, and an investment by the client in transformational goals for his life and work.

It is important that you remember to remain flexible, explore multiple delivery approaches, and be guided by your client's needs and wants. We encourage therapist-trained coaches to consider the variety of potential coaching formats for clients and not to assume that a face-to-face 50-minute session is necessarily the best fit for all life coaching clients.

A life coaching session can occur anywhere that makes sense for the client and the coach. The majority of our current life coaching clients meet with us via the telephone. We also have had face-to-face clients and believe in using multiple contact sources for clients, including letters, faxes, or e-mail in addition to our regular coaching phone calls.

Often therapist-trained coaches are concerned about using formats other than face-to-face sessions. After years of studying and practicing the important aspects of body language (nonverbal behavior, proximity, office arrangement, and so on), it is difficult to imagine a successful helping relationship in any other format. However, we assure you, life coaching over the telephone is an extremely viable format for this particular helping relationship.

We have been asked if there is a qualitative difference between face-to-face life coaching and coaching over the telephone. Our sense is that it depends on the topic and the client. For most situations, the telephone medium works great. For some clients, the anonymity fosters more disclosure than an in-person session would. Coaching over the telephone also works great for busy adults. They can simply close their office door and pick up the telephone for their coaching call instead of having to drive to a life coach's office or another meeting place. Telephone sessions also allow the life coach to take detailed notes, consult resources, and stay focused on what the client is saying without the distractions of nonverbal behaviors and appearance. By contrast, some clients feel more comfortable initially meeting with their coach in person and are more open to sharing their life dreams in the coach's presence. The bottom line involves determining what works best for each client and the level of flexibility you are willing to establish in your practice.

Here are some tips for therapists transitioning to telephone coaching:

1. Take some telecourse coach training courses. These experiences will boost your confidence regarding what you can accomplish over the telephone.
2. Buy the best equipment you can afford. A quality headset is worth every penny you expend for comfort, audio clarity, and the feeling of connectedness with your client.
3. Start slowly. If you have some in-person clients, try coaching them on the phone when they are traveling or having them call from their office for a change of pace. If you plan to have only telephone clients, start with a couple and build up. You will quickly learn to love this medium of communication for its convenience and power. Coaches and clients often comment on the increased anonymity and surprising connection when they feel coaching by phone.
4. Plan to eliminate distractions just as you would if you were seeing the client in person. Stay focused on the client. Just because he or she can't see you doesn't make it wise to open your mail, work on your computer, or play with your dog during a session.
5. Make an agreement with your client to report when either of you has difficulty hearing the other during your call. This removes the anxiety that maybe you aren't picking up all the details of the conversation.

Similar to the location or format of coaching sessions, when and how long coaches and clients meet depend in large part on the needs of each of them. Some coaches prefer a structured format, such as a monthly retainer and weekly half-hour phone calls. However, this is only one format. Other coaches find this much too short a coaching session and prefer 75 minutes or anything in between. Some coaches schedule daily 10-minute telephone check-ins when they are helping clients with specific habit changes. Face-to-face coaching sessions can span days, hours, or even minutes. The options are limitless.

This difference between therapy and coaching provides a whole new sense of openness and opportunity. It permits you to travel and still maintain your schedule or to have international clients and develop a schedule that accommodates both of your needs. The key ingredients are creativity and flexibility. You can create any system that serves your clients and works for you, and you can also change that system over time to everyone's best advantage.

That point leads us right into the next distinction between therapy and coaching—how you get your clients.

## How You Generate New Clients: Limited versus Open

The traditional therapist finds new clients through referral sources and possibly advertisements in the telephone directory or business listings. Therapists with a more entrepreneurial inclination may generate clients through presentations in the community, by teaching a college class, or even via their website. However, as therapists seeking new clients, we generally rely on "soft" approaches, and we often don't market ourselves in the traditional sense. For example, if someone starts to disclose a personal concern at a dinner party, we typically wouldn't say, "Oh, I'd love to be your therapist—I believe I can really help you resolve that problem." But as a coach, the situation changes.

When you get into the same conversation as a life coach, it would be very appropriate to say, "Well, I'd love to coach you on that. I believe you can figure that one out pretty quickly. If you are interested, we could give it a try. Why don't you call me for a complimentary session and we can work on it? Here's my business card." This is not pushy—you're just offering your service to someone who looks like a great new client. It is perfectly ethical and, in fact, the appropriate thing to do if you really believe you can support the individual in reaching his or her life dreams and if you have room in your practice. You can speak more about what you do and go further as a life coach than you can as a therapist trying to gain new therapy clients. In fact, good coaches could ask someone who has described a challenge or life obstacle if he or she would be interested in being coached, right then, for a few minutes on that issue. This powerful interaction demonstrates immediately what life coaching is about rather than trying to find the appropriate words to describe it. As you can imagine, it would be not only difficult but unethical to tell a person that he or she needed to see you in your therapy office!

## Similarities between Therapy and Coaching

Now that we have discussed the differences between therapy and coaching, let's examine some of the transferable skills we believe good therapists bring to the life coaching relationship. Your academic preparation and training as a helping professional—whether as a counselor, social worker, family therapist, psychiatrist, or psychologist—are highly applicable and relevant to the coaching relationship. It is in this area where therapy and coaching are most similar. Over the past 20 years, some schools of therapy have begun to look more like coaching programs. In fact, as we've mentioned, some universities now offer coaching classes as part of their counseling curricula. We also know doctoral students who are doing their dissertations on coaching principles. These endeavors will continue to provide us with enhanced information about the coaching relationship.

Depending on what kind of background you have, much of what you've learned as a therapist or helping professional will serve you well as a life coach. Listening skills, reframing, positive regard for the client, note taking, and process skills are just a few transferable skills. Additionally, you know how to conduct intake interviews and discuss difficult issues with clients, and you have probably heard such a variety of stories in therapy that you won't be surprised with the issues people bring to coaching. If you are trained in solution-focused therapy, which uses questions to focus the client's attention and awareness on what works rather than what is broken, you already have a valuable set of tools you can transfer to life coaching.

☞ TRY IT! ☜

Consider the major therapeutic approaches listed below. In your journal, make a list of the skills, techniques, and strategies you've developed as a therapist that you believe would be valuable in the coaching relationship.

Psychodynamic                 Gestalt therapy
Rogerian/Humanistic           Solution-focused therapy
Cognitive–behavioral          Ericksonian hynotherapy
Behavioral                    Neuro-linguistic programming (NLP)
Developmental                 Psychosynthesis
Positive psychology           Group therapy
Family systems therapy        Add others with which you are familiar

For example, you may have learned from cognitive therapy that it is important to separate thought from emotion. From Ericksonian approaches you may have learned reframing, and your Rogerian training may have taught you the value of unconditional positive regard. All of these are valuable skills to retain for your life coaching practice.

We hope you identified some overlaps between your preparation as a trained helping professional and your work as a life coach. Additional similarities between therapy and coaching extend beyond the transferable skills you, as a trained helping professional, bring to the relationship. These include the following.

Shared Characteristics of Therapy and Coaching

A fee is paid for the service.
The client wants to change.
You are in a professional helper role.
It is an ongoing, confidential, typically one-to-one relationship.
The dialogue between you and the client is the primary vehicle for
    delivering the service.

*continued on next page*

Listening is perhaps the most critical skill upon which your success depends.

The relationship can be group-based.

The sessions are regularly scheduled.

There is an assumption that change occurs over a period of time.

## ☞ TRY IT! ☜

This is an exercise we often do with therapists who transition to life coaching. We believe it is very important to examine and be up front about the assumptions you currently hold about clients and the helping relationship. These come from years of education, training, and practice.

*Step 1.* Ask yourself the following question: "What are some of the key assumptions I've developed as a therapist about the following topics?" Use your journal to record your responses.

1. The therapeutic relationship.
2. The clients I see.
3. The way I get clients.

*Step 2.* Thinking about some of the distinctions between therapy and life coaching we've discussed in this chapter, review what you just wrote and ask yourself, "What are some of the assumptions I've made about myself and my role as a helper that I need to examine because they may not fit for coaching?"

For example, another common therapeutic assumption is that something is wrong or broken and needs "fixing" in the client's life. Coaches do not make this assumption, but instead assume that the client is whole and not in need of repair.

*Step 3.* Take time to examine and record your assumptions and what you discovered about them in your journal. Here's an example: "I discovered that I often feel pressure to be the expert in the helping relationship. I always feel as though I should know the answer and that the client is looking to me for the solutions. I don't like this feeling because much of the time I really believe the client knows better than I where he or she should go from here."

When Deb teaches workshops, she often describes changing our therapeutic assumptions to the coaching perspective as analogous to resetting the default buttons on your computer. In therapy, we've been trained to function from a certain operating system. As you begin to transition into the coaching perspective and operate from coaching assumptions, it is necessary to reset the default buttons on your own internal operating system so that you can think and act like a coach rather than as a therapist.

As the coaching profession evolves, we develop increasing awareness of the distinctions and similarities between therapy and coaching. Therapists are learning that we have many transferable skills and appropriate preparation that serve us well as we transition from helping professionals to life coaches. However, we also recognize that the two relationships are distinctive and some of the assumptions we've made as therapists are not appropriate in the life coaching relationship. It is your obligation as a professional who wants to become a great life coach to recognize and modify or eliminate the assumptions and practices that may stand in the way of success for your coaching clients.

## How to Make the Distinctions Work

Some of you may have discovered that the education and training you've received have led you to develop strong therapeutic assumptions and practices that differ significantly from what will best serve you in life coaching. You will need to consciously reframe or drop some traditional behavior, and learn some new ones.

For others, the shift will not seem so great. Consider this comment from Roz Van Meter, one of our workshop participants and a graduate of the Institute for Life Coach Training:

> With regard to the transition from therapist to coach, for some of us, the step is small. The transition is really not tough. Those of us who have been doing Gestalt-type "how" rather than "why" therapy for years and who are very outcome-oriented in their counseling and not

stuck in the medical model negotiate this transition swiftly, especially if we are accustomed to working for fees only. We find no trouble distinguishing between therapy and coaching because we've been doing coaching for years in our offices and just calling it therapy.

What is most important is that you recognize the differences between therapy and coaching, understand and acknowledge your assumptions that may interfere with the life coaching relationship, and take action to minimize and eliminate any potential interference. Here are some suggestions to help you make the distinctions work.

- *Do not use the "why" question.* A common assumption many therapists hold is that they must understand the "why" of clients' actions to help them change their behavior. Therapists learn this orientation early in their training. In coaching, this assumption could not be further from the truth. One very successful life coach, Sherry Lowry, advises new coaches who have a helping professional background to stop themselves in the coaching conversation if they hear themselves moving into the why. She even goes so far as to recommend that they excuse themselves for a few seconds to clear their head, get out of the therapy mindset, and get back into the coaching perspective.
- *Change your therapeutic habits into coaching habits.* Much of our conduct in therapy is comprised of learned behavior and habits. These can be changed with intention and practice. Look at the list of assumptions that you thought might get in your way as a coach. Identify two of them and start working on them today. As we discussed in the previous chapter, use a system to monitor your progress and, if possible, work with a colleague to help reinforce each other's change.

   Some therapists transitioning into life coaching use 3 × 5 cards attached to their computer or telephone to remind themselves of the distinctions between life coaching assumptions or behaviors and their traditional therapeutic way of operating. For example, one coach we know has a bright florescent 3 × 5 card taped to her computer that says: "Get out of the past and into the future." Another's reads" "The client is brilliant, not you." A third person's says: "Listen for the WANTS." It is important that you find individual ways to help yourself stay focused in the life coaching model rather than the therapeutic model.

- *Celebrate your transferable skills.* When we learn something new, we tend to forget all the basic, helpful practices we already use. We often find that therapists who want to be life coaches forget all the great skills they already have. These are the gifts and talents that put you out ahead of the nontherapist–trained coach who is going to need to learn how to listen effectively before even beginning to coach. Recognize and celebrate what you bring to this new learning, including your intuition, listening skills, and reframing abilities.

Additional suggestions to help you further develop a coaching perspective include the following:

1. *Stay with us and we'll help you.* Finish this book. We will coach you through the transition and help you further clarify the differences and similarities between therapy and coaching throughout the book.
2. *Get a therapist-trained mentor coach.* If you are serious about wanting to make a transition into life coaching, a mentor coach can help you mark the path. We recommend you hire a mentor coach who has successfully transitioned from therapy.
3. *Sign up for a reputable and qualified coach-training course.* The ICF keeps on their website (*www.coachfederation.org*) an updated list of all coach training programs that have attained the status of Accredited Coach Training Programs (ACTP) and completed a rigorous audit of the quality of their content and processes for teaching coaching skills. Many other organizations teach coaching, and some may be high quality, but you can be assured by training at an ICF-recognized school. Each one is listed with details of their method of teaching and training, theoretical models, and their ideal student, as well as the financial and time investment necessary.

The following table summarizes the major distinctions between therapy and coaching. David Steele, our colleague and a former member of the faculty at the Institute for Life Coach Training, assisted us early on to further delineate the similarities and differences between the two fields. His work has been instrumental in developing the tables we have provided. Some of the characteristics listed in the table are beyond the scope of this book and are more applicable to a full coach-training program. However, Table 4.1 will help you develop your own understanding of ways in which the two professions differ.

**Table 4.1** Therapy vs. Coaching

| THERAPY | COACHING |
|---|---|
| ***Focus*** | |
| Relieve pain, symptoms | Attain specific goals, desires |
| Restore functioning, adjustment | Create personal fulfillment |
| History, past | Vision, future |
| "Why?" | "How?" |
| Patient wants to move away from pain | Client wants to move toward goals that are attractive |
| ***Context*** | |
| Medical/clinical model | Educational/developmental model |
| Diagnosable illness | Desirable goals, life transitions, or personal growth |
| Paradigm of pathology | Paradigm of possibility |
| ***Relationship*** | |
| Therapist as expert; client as patient | Coach as cocreator; a partnership of equals |
| ***Orientation*** | |
| Orientation is process: feelings and inner world | Orientation is outcome, action: inner to outer worlds |
| ***Responsibility*** | |
| Therapist is responsible for process, direction, outcomes | Coach is responsible for process; client, for results |
| ***Style*** | |
| Limited (if any) personal disclosure | Personal disclosure okay as an aid to learning |
| Forwards the work through healing, reparenting, emotions, catharsis | Forwards the work through action, talents, strengths, behaviors, insight into action |

In summary, it is critical that therapists who transition to life coaching understand the distinctions between the two professions. Your previous training and experiences will dictate how far you need to go in order to obtain the coaching perspective.

Pat Williams created Table 4.2 to further delineate distinctions and similarities between coaching and other professions.

**Table 4.2** Therapy vs. Coaching and Other Professions

| Therapy | Mentoring | Consulting | Coaching |
|---------|-----------|------------|----------|
| Deals mostly with a person's past and trauma, and seeks healing | Deals mostly with succession training and seeks to help someone do what you do | Deals mostly with problems and seeks to provide information (expertise, strategy, structures, methodologies) to solve them | Deals mostly with a person's present and seeks to guide him/her into a more desirable future |
| Doctor–patient relationship (therapist has the answers) | "Older/wiser"–younger/less-experienced relationship (mentor has the answers) | Expert–person with problem relationship (consultant has the answers) | Cocreative equal partnership (Coach helps client discover his/her own answers) |
| Assumes emotions are a symptom of something wrong | Is limited to emotional response of the mentoring parameters (succession, etc.) | Does not normally address or deal with emotions (informational only) | Assumes emotions are natural and normalizes them |
| The therapist diagnoses, then provides professional expertise and guidelines to give you a path to healing | The mentor allows you to observe his/her behavior and expertise, answers questions, provides guidance and wisdom for the stated purpose of the mentoring | The consultant stands back, evaluates a situation, then tells you the problem and how to fix it | The coach stands with you, and helps you identify the challenges, then works with you to turn challenges into victories and holds you accountable to reach your desired goals |

Lastly, Pat offers this analogy, which came to him while teaching a series of seminars along the eastern coast of Australia. While in Brisbane, Pat and his wife Jill rented a car to drive 50 miles to visit Pat's nephew Zachary, who was living in Byron Bay at the time, south of Brisbane, a bohemian type community with a beautiful coastline, artists, and funky galleries and restaurants. This was only the second time that Pat had driven a car with the steering wheel on the right (for him, wrong) side of the car and the driving lane on the left side of the street. (He had rented a car before in New Zealand while vacationing with his two daughters, Megan and Briana, but the roads there were very uncrowded and you had to worry more about sheep than other cars!)

The insight that came to him on this brief car trip was this:

I have been driving since age 15 (40 years at the time of this journey) and I knew all the rules of the road, how the car works, etc., but driving a car in Australia, many things were opposite. The skills were the same, the eye–hand coordination, the mechanics, and the rules of the road were all very much the same, but it was on the WRONG side of the road, and the steering wheel was on the WRONG side of the car! I soon realized that *this* is what it is like to transition from a career of therapy, counseling, ministry, or some other helping profession to coaching. The skills are all similar, but there is a period of discomfort *driving in the other lane*. Coaching feels different yet familiar, just like driving in Australia felt. But you do get used to it, and you do become comfortable after some experience, even if you do go the wrong way in a roundabout into oncoming traffic once in a while.

<< CHAPTER FIVE >>

# Reclaiming Your Soul:
## *The Joyfulness of Life Coaching*

*The most visible joy can only reveal itself to us*
*when we've transformed it within.*
—Rainier Maria Rilke

Many therapists and counselors, especially those in private practice, have seen a monumental shift in the profession in the last several decades. Counseling and psychotherapy were, in our opinion, never meant to be part of the medical model, but were seen by many as an art in relating and helping people overcome psychological obstacles in their lives. But somewhere along the line, the therapy profession was included in third-party payment of services by insurance companies. This practice allowed health insurance to cover psychotherapy if a medical (psychiatric) diagnosis was given to the patient. Most therapists did not even use the term *patient* but instead opted for *client*, lending more credence to the professional view of therapy as a nonmedical service. The more we as a profession co-opted to be part of the medical/psychiatric community, the more entangled we became in the managed care system that began infiltrating the profession in the 1980s and then became extremely intrusive in the 1990s. Almost every practitioner has seen his or her income drastically reduced and paperwork time increased. (The exception here is the practitioner who was "managed care free" and had a large-enough client pool to survive, and even thrive, with fee-for-service clients at a reasonable professional fee.)

This shift to managed care has caused great chaos, consternation, and burnout among private practitioners, to the point where an approximate 10% leave the profession each year and another 10% wish they could! In fact, *Psychotherapy Finances*, in its annual survey of practitioners, states that 23% are taking steps to leave their practice (Klein, 2000). Nineteen percent now list coaching as a service they offer. We might say that coaching was a professional service waiting to happen, and managed care helped it along!

When training therapists about adding coaching to their repertoire, we have both observed and experienced the powerful impact this career transition (whether part-time or full-time) has had. Once clinicians hear about the possibility of working with high-functioning, highly motivated clients who are willing to pay for coaching services, they become filled with excitement and get a joyful expression on their face. After all, most of us never wanted to work with severely depressed or conflicted persons 100% of the time. Didn't you often hope that potential clients would call you because they just wanted to improve their life? Adding coaching as a new skill set allows you to choose more carefully the clients you see for therapy and attract new clients who are candidates for coaching.

As we describe the coaching relationship and the joyfulness of being someone's personal coach, let us first acknowledge that this joyfulness can also be part of the therapeutic relationship. Both of us have provided counseling or psychotherapy for years, and we know that great joy and gratitude can be gained from assisting someone to overcome severe trauma or emotional struggles. We became therapists to have a significant, positive impact on people's lives and relationships. However, three undeniable factors seem to be at work in the profession of psychotherapy that can lead to a less-than-joyful experience for the therapist.

1. *Length of time in the profession*. Psychotherapy with emotionally fragile persons can be draining over the long haul. It is a profession in which the therapists give so much of themselves that burnout results if they do not self-nurture regularly.
2. *The degree of seriousness of clients' issues*. Therapists who often treat clients with serious and complicated diagnoses are more at risk of

burnout due to the psychic and emotional energy required to deal with such difficult and often unresolvable situations.

3. *Managed care.* Therapists who are trapped in the managed care system have fewer "approved" sessions with their clients and a lesser amount of reimbursement, as well as a reduction in income, more hours of paperwork, and increased liability. This scenario has led to a large percentage of private therapists looking for ways to make a living in cash-only practices and needing to add other income streams to their business. Life coaching is a natural transition that can be added, along with training, speaking, and consulting.

## What Makes the Coaching Relationship So Full of Joyful Energy?

Isn't it logical that helping someone to experience a better life—a more fulfilling and empowered existence—should foster the experience of joy both for the helper and the helpee? This is a unique quality of the coaching relationship: The energy exchange seems to be less draining on a coach than it often is on a therapist. In fact, we say if the coaching relationship is draining to you as the coach, you are either working too hard on the client's behalf, or the client is not really coachable and may need therapy. We address this situation more explicitly in the next chapter.

Many of our colleagues, as well as graduates of our training program who have shifted from therapist to coach, report several factors that have led to a more joyful work experience: the work schedule, the ability to live and work wherever you desire, the egalitarian aspect of the coaching relationship, and the financial rewards. We consider each of these factors next.

### The Work Schedule

Coaches can include a mix of face-to-face coaching and phone coaching, and those who do phone coaching can work from home or wherever they happen to be. There are no parking concerns and no need to dress up. Coaches with international clients can even adjust their work hours to accommodate time-zone differences, thereby increasing their market base to global potential. One former therapist, Barbara Blocker, says,

I no longer try to fit into somebody else's system or rules about how something needs to be done. I feel good about that because I can control what I do, and it fits who I am. I can control my schedule so that it fits my personal life, and the balance between work, play, and family is wonderful.

This statement reflects what we have heard from other coaches. You can still be part of your local community and meet people face to face, but your playing field expands to the whole world when you work by phone and e-mail. You still feel very connected with your clients and they with you.

### Ability to Live and Work Wherever You Desire

Coaches who work by telephone, with occasional in-person sessions, can live in desirous places where building a therapy practice would have been difficult (unless one does therapy primarily by phone, to which we have serious objections and which leads to more liability concerns as well). We know coaches who live in very remote communities, on boats, and even in RVs for periods of time. Telecoaching is not geographically constrained. Some coaches have even exchanged homes with another coach for a month, and the only professional adjustment was to give their clients a different phone number for that period. Our joy of coaching comes, in part, from the opportunity to live, work, and play anywhere and maintain a professional presence and above-average income as well. The following story from Christopher McCluskey is a great example of this possibility:

Coaching has been my ticket to an almost entirely different way of life! Lest that statement sound too grandiose, understand that I used to live in a densely populated section of Tampa Bay and had a thriving private practice with a staff of therapists and interns. I was at the office Monday through Friday and saw my family in the evenings and on weekends.

I now live on 440 acres in the foothills of the Ozark Mountains on a little dirt road where the nearest town's population is 215. I do my coaching out of a hunter's cabin I converted into an office, and I work entirely by telephone, e-mail, and fax machine. I eat all my meals at home, interacting with my wife and children (who are home-schooled) throughout the day.

Coaching clients all over the world, I have a flexibility and freedom that never would have been possible in my old practice. I do much of my coaching from the deck of my office, watching the children and horses, petting the dogs, and enjoying the fresh air. I have coached "on the road" while taking field trips with the family, and taught a teleclass series while on vacation this summer at a beach house.

Life in the country was a dream for our family, and coaching is what made it possible. I never could have had a private practice out here and, even if I commuted to the nearest town of any size, I'd still be gone the entire day and very tied to the office. Add to that the stress and liability of full-time therapy work, and I can only say that I wish I'd made this transition earlier! I am more fulfilled and joyful than I have ever been in my life.

### Egalitarian Aspect of the Coaching Relationship

Psychotherapy and counseling require, or at least assume, a hierarchical aspect to the relationship. Therapy takes on a doctor–patient or expert–client context and requires strict boundaries and ethics in the relationship outside of the office. In the coaching relationship, the concerns of transference and counter-transference are not part of the equation. Although our professional training as therapists certainly makes us sensitive to that construct, we are much freer to be ourselves and be more authentic with our clients. At a time when Pat's wife lost her hearing in one ear due to a sudden and severe bout with meningitis, he shared that situation with his clients when he had to take a week off to be with her in a nearby hospital. (Many therapists might also share in this way but with more caution and perhaps less detail.) When coaching resumed afterward, many clients asked about Pat's wife, and how he was doing as well. One client (an attorney) shared with Pat how much he appreciated "seeing the person behind the coach." The relationship actually became richer because of the ability to be real. Another therapist-turned-coach, Carol Gaffney, says this:

As a therapist, you meet some wonderful people, but once they were your client, they could not be your friend, and if you met them in public it was always a little strained. But as a coach, I am able to meet wonderful people, know them, and have them know me. We can have lunch, we can have coffee, and we can have a relationship that is not a therapeutic relationship. It is a professional relationship that is also a caring relationship, and relationships are the basis of business success.

Another coach, Judi Craig, says:

Coaching is an interdevelopmental relationship where you come together as two equals. I think that although some therapists were comfortable with self-disclosure in therapy sessions, in coaching, clients certainly can know much more about your life and your experiences. This disclosure can even be part of good coaching.

## Financial Rewards

Although we realize that money is not the driving factor in all careers, we also believe that as therapists we have been undervalued and underpaid relative to our expertise, training, and effort. So, the fact that life coaching can command a higher hourly fee or monthly retainer than therapy and requires no third-party billing is very inviting. To us, money that is appropriate to the value received for the client is very freeing and more in line with other professions, such as accounting, legal services, strategic planning, and public relations. Professions that provide great value and results should command good fees.

We believe that in recent times professional therapists, on average, have been making less money but working more hours. For therapists dependent on third-party payers and managed care rules, hourly fees have dropped and paperwork has increased. Even those who are in a private practice may have trouble commanding fees higher than $100 per hour. Of course, exceptions exist in large metropolitan cities, but basically this is an average fee. Although some coaching clients may not have the resources to pay more than that, most coaches command fees from $100 to $300 per hour—sometimes more for corporate or executive coaching. Coaching is generally intended for people who are already successful and who view coaching as something valuable to assist them in achieving more, making big changes, and living the life they really want.

# Reclaiming Your Soul

Now that we have discussed the four points that lead to joyfulness in coaching, here are personalized comments from some of our colleagues who have recently trained to be coaches.

"Coaching is my love!! Coaching has been about the power of transformation in my life and in the lives of my clients. It is truly a gift to be a part of my clients' journeys to the awareness of the innermost part of their being—to the inner sanctuary of their soul. It is there, deep in the soul, where they find peace and joy. It is there that they find their own sacredness, where they know the joy of living and the joy of loving self and others. It is there that they find the passion of living their lives! As they learn the power of their thoughts and the power of intention and visioning, their personal and professional lives are transformed as their dreams are manifested. My life has been changed from one of just existing in a day-to-day routine of work and chores to a life filled with gratitude, celebration, and joy."

"My 24-year-old son was killed in November 1998, and the grief stripped me of my energy, resourcefulness, and joy. I stopped taking new therapy clients and, as the people I was treating got better or moved, my practice dwindled. I did not have the attention to details or tolerance for other people's pain necessary to tackle new cases with my usual fervor and enthusiasm. Since I usually gave 200% of myself, my clients still got good therapy when it dropped to 100%, but I felt drained and compromised. When I went to hear Pat present coaching for a day, I felt excited for the first time in years. Within a month, I was in class. Coaching helped me to continue my professional career in a more positive, forward-moving fashion. I have named my business DreamCatchers after the Indian tradition: If you hang a dreamcatcher over your bed, it will only let the good dreams through. I know I can't keep tragic things from happening, but I can keep them from spoiling my dreams. I have renewed my life purpose: to touch souls deeply while honoring mine. Grief stripped me of my purpose, and coaching is giving it back. There is no better definition of joy."

"Through coaching and coach training, I have learned to live more in the present. I have noticed that when I am canoeing, as I literally stop thinking or worrying about what is around the next corner, I am more aware of the color of the sky, the warm sun and wind against my cheek, the scenery I am passing, the sound of the birds, the water, the branches blown by the wind, or the canoe moving through the water. This has become a metaphor for my life: When I am not so concerned about what is around the next bend, my awareness and joy in the present moment increase tenfold. Also, rediscovering what I am passionate about helps guide me down the path, providing direction."

"My greatest happiness in coaching—the one that carries over long after the session ends—is guiding clients to discover their life purpose and the manner in which they will best use the many talents and gifts they have. It's like seeing them choose the ideal destination for the most significant trip of their lives. After they know where they are going, the path becomes infinitely clearer, the obstacles more manageable, and their own journey much more enjoyable!

"This process is especially meaningful for me when I work with midlife clients who have already explored several options but are experiencing a heartfelt longing for a more satisfying life. When they discover what it is that they are intended to do, when they become acutely aware that their lives have a rich and deep purpose, their happiness is almost palpable. And because it is so contagious, I get to share in their feelings of abundance. It is truly a blessing to behold—and I feel honored to be part of the process."

"My first client really made me want to continue on with life coaching instead of therapy. In 90 minutes I saw a woman in her early 50s change from being so depressed and hopeless to having so many new ideas of possibilities that she didn't know what to do first. This does not happen in therapy. A couple days later, she realized she had been depressed for two years and that our talk had turned around her whole life. She had all these ideas stored in her head, but no one ever wanted to listen to her or encourage her to go for her dreams. Like her, I realize that life just keeps getting better and better. God only knows where I am going, but I sure enjoy the journey."

For those who are not currently in private practice and who work for a school, clinic, employee-assistance program, or elsewhere, we recommend that you try the above exercise with your colleagues as well as those who are your clients in whatever setting. View everyone you encounter this week as brilliant and capable of greatness. Imagine how differently you would act if you viewed everyone in this way.

Are you excited about reclaiming your passion and experiencing more joy in your work and in your client relationships? We believe that adding coaching to your business is a great way to live as you want and help others to live as they want. What could be better? And you can even continue to see therapy clients, but on your terms. Therapy might become more fulfilling, and your clients might experience you and your energy in a whole new way!

---

## ☞ TRY IT! ☜

If you are still in a therapy practice, let's examine how this might look. Imagine one of your clients, and assume that he or she is capable of greatness and transformation. Hold that belief despite the degree of that client's disturbance, or the level of his or her trauma. Imagine how you might act or work differently with this client if you were his or her life coach, rather than therapist. Imagine assisting this client to uncover his or her unique brilliance. How does it feel? What what you do differently?

Even with clinically diagnosable therapy clients, we believe that the paradigm of coaching and the context of the coaching relationship fosters a potentially more rewarding experience for the therapist, and probably for the client as well. What do you think?

Let's examine the coaching relationship in greater detail, and explore some of the key ingredients of a successful life coaching relationhip.

---

# CHAPTER SIX

# The Life Coaching Relationship

*I believe we can change the world if we start listening to one
another again . . . simple, honest, human conversation.*
— Margaret J. Wheatley

The life coaching relationship is like a dance. It starts with an introduction
and moves to increasing levels of intimacy. At the first meeting, the coach
usually "leads" by helping the potential client learn the basics and practice a
few life coaching steps. Some distance between partners is common as the
dance begins; the coach works to establish the ingredients and principles
necessary for a successful and deepening relationship.

As the dance continues and intimacy increases, the client takes the lead
and the dance can take many forms. Sometimes it is a waltz, slow and clearly
delineated. At other times, it feels more like a tango with staccato steps and
a fast beat. Perhaps it is rock 'n roll with loud background music and a driving
beat that moves both coach and client forward. Whatever the dance,
remember that once the relationship is established, the client should always
lead the dance. She picks the music, sets the tempo, and initiates the steps.
The life coach helps her stay on the dance floor and encourages her exploration of new steps. This dance and relationship can go on for years, sustained
by the client's commitment to seek the life of her dreams and the coach's
commitment to help her achieve it. Over time this relationship grows and
deepens as the two dancers move masterfully into the future.

## Ingredients of a Successful Life Coaching Relationship

Now that you have an understanding of the distinctions and similarities between therapy and coaching, and a sense of the joyfulness in your practice, we would like to discuss life coaching relationships. As more is being written about coaching in general and life coaching in particular, we have multiple models and structures for the coaching relationship.

Similarly, the language of coaching is growing and expanding as the field develops. Phrases such as *holding the client's agenda, coaching from the inside out, adding value, forwarding the action,* and *the client is brilliant* permeate coaches' conversations and can be found in dialogue at most coaching gatherings and in many coach training manuals. (Many of these terms are defined later in the book.) Just as the language of counseling became commonplace through the usage of counselors, so too is the language of coaching moving through our profession and the general public. So many people are inventing and using new phrases, and ideas are so openly exchanged, that it is almost impossible to determine who said what first.

We want you, as a therapist considering life coaching, to have a sense of the foundational pieces of the life coaching relationship. Similar to what we learned in courses on foundations of counseling, or foundations of therapy, several ingredients are essential for an effective coaching relationship to occur. For the purpose of this book, we present what we believe are the necessary ingredients for the spark to occur in the life coaching dance. Not all coach training programs encourage this type of relationship, and that is fine. Positive outcomes and good things may happen in coaching without these ingredients. However, from the way we teach and train, we believe that the following components are significant contributors to a successful life coaching relationship:

1. The focus is the person's whole life.
2. The coaching environment is a safe place in which the client can grow.
3. The truth is always told.
4. There is a reserved space, just for the client.
5. The possibilities are limitless.
6. The relationship is soulful.

Let's examine each of these in the context of the life coaching relationship.

## The Focus Is the Person's Whole Life

Ellis (1998) and Whitworth et al. (1998) have both written about coaching from a whole-life perspective. The assumption is that clients don't live their lives in boxes of work, health, relationships, and so on, even though they might say they do. Whatever is going on in one aspect of clients' lives impacts other areas of their being. Once clients begin to see this interaction, they gain a wider view of their lives and become more thoughtful about the decisions they make.

It is our opinion that coaches do clients a disservice when they help them excel in one aspect of their lives while ignoring the rest. From our teaching and training perspective, focusing on the whole-life is critical. This is why we call our work "life coaching" rather than business coaching, relationship coaching, or some other title.

To this end, we recommend that our therapist-trained coaches use some type of whole life assessment in their early sessions with a client, usually after establishing rapport and forming trust. The specific type of assessment is not as important as the product it produces.

Whole-life assessment permits the coach to see how the client evaluates his or her level of satisfaction in significant areas of a balanced life, including career, health, finances, relationship, spirituality, personal growth (including intellectual and emotional), leisure, family, and continuing education.

Clients benefit simply from acknowledging that they *do* have a whole life. We often see clients who are stuck on one part of life, such as work, but blind to the other aspects of their lives and how they interrelate. When coaches help them see things from a whole-life perspective, clients are often amazed to discover how some pieces have been neglected or pushed aside.

## The Coaching Environment Is a Safe Place
## in which the Client Can Grow

If it were easy for our clients to accomplish all their life dreams, they would not need us. Life coaching clients want a place where they can approach the life they have created to this point with the optimism to see new opportunities, faith in their ability to implement effective change, and the courage to move into the future and take steps toward the life of their dreams.

As trained therapists, we know that clients are most successful when they feel safe with their helper, and this is certainly the case with life coaching. If our clients are going to take huge risks in order to make significant changes in their life, they need to trust that they have a safe place from which to leave and return. A life coaching relationship is that safe place. Two factors critical to a sense of safety are confidentiality and trust.

Confidentiality is nothing new to therapist-trained life coaches. We know that if clients are going to talk freely about their life and their goals, they need to know when, if ever, their coach might disclose the content of their conversations. Just like a therapy intake, it is important during your coaching intake to explain any limitations to confidentiality to the client. At the time of this writing, privileged communication is not granted to coaches, and we do not expect that to be the case in the near future. Therapists planning to maintain dual practices (both therapy and coaching) should further investigate confidentiality issues with their insurance carriers and state licensing boards.

You also know the vital role that trust plays in any helping relationship. We show clients we are trustworthy by showing up on time for calls and following through with our promises. We also empower clients with trust by holding them responsible for following through on what they say they want. Clients learn that we are on their side, want for them only what they want, and trust them to get it. Trusting our clients' wants provides them with a safe, encouraging environment from which to go forth and take on the huge life changes they want to make.

## Truth Is Always Told

Sometimes in life it seems hard to find truthful people, even in our most intimate partnerships. In life coaching relationships, the truth is always told. From the first intake session, the life coach and client agree to be completely honest with one another.

Effective life coaches want to hear the truth from clients because they know that is when real learning occurs. Clients want to share celebrations and mistakes in a nonjudgmental, safe, and trustworthy place. Clients count on life coaches to tell them the truth and help them sort through the craziness of life's concerns. Authentic coaching demands that the coach be real and not hold back or just accept what the client is saying. We teach something we call *compassionate edge*, a coaching skill that allows the coach to be truthful but not mean or uncaring. In therapy we are often aware of the fragility of our clients, and we try to be cautious with our truth telling. In coaching, we are tactful and gently direct; we do not cushion our words so much that their meaning is lost. Instead, we act as a mirror for the client to see how he is acting and what he is doing. For example, a coach might say: "I've noticed that for the last three weeks you've told me you are going to get a replacement for your administrative assistant. Yet every week you come to our call complaining about being overloaded and overwhelmed at work. When are you going to do something about the replacement? Do you want to develop a plan for that today, or is it no longer a priority for you?"

Clients are often aware of how they conceal their truth from others, and they aren't paying their life coach to be treated in the same fashion. Gentle, loving confrontation is part of the effective life coach's tool kit. This does not imply that life coaches tell clients what they should or shouldn't do; instead, they remind them of what *they* said they wanted. This is a relationship without judgment.

## There Is a Reserved Space Just for the Client

Life coaching clients really appreciate that the coaching relationship provides a time "just for me." In this crazy world of multitasking, where people do two or three things at the same time and feel good about it, slowing down to focus on what you really want out of life seems a rarity. In fact, it is one of the benefits our clients most appreciate about life coaching. Knowing that once a week they will be contacting their coach and receiving full attention on their visions and concerns (their hopes, dreams, fears, wants, frustrations, irritations, and sorrows) is seen as a tremendous gift. This time for the client is similar to the space clients create in their lives for therapy.* A difference is

---

*This is also one of the reasons why many people seek the services of a therapist.

that, in all cases, the coaching client wants this time and has requested it. Coaching relationships are voluntary—never mandated by an outside source, the way some therapeutic relationships may be. This difference allows clients to savor the space they have created for themselves and enjoy their own growth.

## Possibilities Are Limitless

Clients direct the life coaching agenda and can bring up anything they wish during a life coaching session. There is room for their dreams and wants in all aspects of their life—from the immediate present to the far-distant future. This space is so huge that at first some clients can't comprehend the powerful possibilities awaiting them. Life coaches are available to assist clients in figuring out multiple pathways to achieve what they really want. Clients' wants may include cleaning their closets, doubling their income, resolving a conflict with an employee, enhancing intimacy with their spouse, creating a positive relationship with their teenager, leaving a legacy, or planning for retirement in three years. Rarely do we ever hear of a client honestly wanting something that isn't in his or her best interest. If this were to occur, we'd simply discuss the situation openly with the client. In fact, the opposite will more likely occur. Clients usually create such big dreams and huge wants that the coach can become breathless keeping up with them. There is room for giant wants and bodacious dreams in the life coaching relationship.

## The Relationship Is Soulful

We believe that great life coaching goes beyond the surface of the relationship, the techniques, or the day-to-day to-do lists. We are especially attracted to what Dave Ellis (1998) refers to as soulful life coaching. We believe the life coaching relationship is, at its best, soulful.

Now, we recognize that not all coaching relationships are soulful. In fact, some coaches, particularly those not trained in the helping professions, might even find this type of relationship uncomfortable and unappealing. It is fine with us that some coaches prefer to operate at a more basic level. Perhaps they are most comfortable working with clients on more surface-level issues such as management problems, organizational concerns, and time management. We believe all of these are significant, and some of our clients work on these areas in their life coaching relationships with us. However, we want our therapist-trained life coaches to reach for a deeper, more soulful relationship with their clients. Life coaches who were prepared as therapists are uniquely poised to enter into powerful relationships with their clients. When the coach and client enter into a deep and meaningful relationship, great things happen—in fact, miracles can occur. People have totally transformed or recreated their lives. Long-forgotten dreams have found their way into reality. Coaching is about possibilities, and the coaching relationship is fertile ground where everyday life can be improved and dreams can grow.

## Powerful Life Coaching Principles

Beyond the six significant ingredients of a successful life coaching relationship we have just presented, we would like to offer three powerful life coaching principles that guide our work as life coaches:

1. We believe that our clients are whole and brilliant (even when they don't act that way).
2. We believe that clients want what they say they want (even when they don't act as though they do).
3. We believe that we are partners and cocreators with clients to help them get what they want.

Let's examine each of these principles individually.

### *Clients Are Whole and Capable*
### *(Even When They Don't Act That Way)*

During our training as helping professionals, we are taught that clients bring an identifiable "problem." The perspective is that something is "broken" and we, as therapists, need to help "fix" the problem through our wisdom, experiences, and answers. We hold the keys that help unlock doors and free clients from their discomfort. As therapists we were taught that we have the skills, knowledge, and expertise to help solve clients' issues. Even when we didn't intend to be in the role of problem solver, we often saw clients as needing us to help them find their way. Our strategy typically would be to help clients discover and understand what is broken or not working before we moved on to help them look at possible resolutions to the problem.

Life coaches see clients as whole, with nothing wrong, broken, missing, or in need of repair. We also believe that only clients have the answers to their concerns. Therefore, we encourage clients to examine what they really want and to explore possible ways they might start moving forward to achieve their goals. We wouldn't concern ourselves (as we would in therapy) with what hasn't been working that kept them from getting what they wanted earlier. Rather, we help clients move into the future and create multiple pathways to reach their goals.

For example, if a client were discouraged about his weight, we would want to know his life history and explore how long and why he has had this weight problem, any family problems with weight, any medical factors, and what he has done up until now to try to lose weight. We would accept that he knows what he wants and ask him what he would like to do that might help him reach the goal of losing weight. We do not concern ourselves with why he hasn't started on this goal earlier (past vs. future) even though he keeps saying he wants it. We support him as he considers what it would look like to reach that goal and as he examines various ways he might work to achieve what he wants. Depending on the client, we might teach him how to manage weight loss with a general fitness program and help him discover ways to monitor his progress and celebrate his successes. Solution-focused therapists will recognize some overlap in this example between their training and the coaching paradigm.

We know from our own life coaching experiences that even when clients don't think they have the answer, they do. We've also learned that if we stand by our clients with full belief in their brilliance, they will not only find what they are seeking but will also feel better about themselves because they discovered the answers themselves. This attitude reinforces their self-esteem, confidence, and solution-finding abilities, while also increasing the likelihood that they will follow through on solutions of their own creation.

Certainly some clients have a desire for someone else to find their solutions or fix their challenges. However, after years of life coaching, we are absolutely clear that coaches do their clients a disservice by recommending specific solutions or strategies. As the old saying goes: "Give a man a fish, feed him for a day. Teach a man to fish, feed him for a lifetime."

We recommend that coaches always help clients create multiple strategies or solutions to get what they want and achieve their goals, thereby encouraging self-exploration and discovery. Consider the following exchange:

COACH: What would you like to work on today?

CLIENT: I'm so stressed out! I want to do something about my office—it's driving me crazy!!

COACH: What do you want to do?

CLIENT: I want to clean it up. I can't find anything!

COACH: Okay, you want to clean up your office so you can find what you are looking for. Is that it?

CLIENT: Yes, that would help a lot. I'd feel better and get more done.

COACH: Great, you can have that! What can you do to clean your office so you can find what you are looking for?

CLIENT: I could toss this pile of magazines, journals, and junk mail that I haven't gotten around to reading.

COACH: Okay, what else?

CLIENT: I could put these project binders on the bookshelf in my closet and get them up off the floor where I always trip over them.

COACH: That sounds like it will help you out. What else?

CLIENT: Hmm, I need a good place to put my mail when it comes in, especially my bills, so I can be sure to pay them on time.

COACH: Okay, what else can you do besides tossing the piles of magazines, moving the project binders, and creating a regular place for mail and bills? Would that help you reach your goal of being able to find things in your office and thereby reduce some of this stress?

When clients are encouraged and supported to look inside themselves for solutions and strategies, they learn about themselves, their strengths, and their limitations. We agree with Dave Ellis, who says, "Life coaching is about people generating their own answers, not looking outside of themselves for solutions" (1998, p. 3).

Through the life coaching process, clients also discover what they want, what motivates them, what scares them, and when they sell themselves short. Many times clients create a solution and think that it is the one. How many times have you known someone who thinks he or she has the answer, only to realize it does not work when applied to the particular situation? Helping clients create multiple pathways to reach their goals supports them in reaching those goals armed with many different tools and the confidence that they can create additional options if needed.

### Clients Want What They Say They Want
### (Even When They Don't Act As Though They Do)

Similar to believing that our clients are whole and capable of getting what they want in their lives, we believe them when they tell us what they want—even if the want might initially surprise us.

When we do a whole-life survey with our clients, we discover what they want in many areas of their lives. From that point forward, they keep adding to their wants. We keep a list of what they want in our notes and remind them of what they have said. Even if they tell us a want in December and haven't done anything about it in June, we still believe they want it. For example, let's assume in December a client says she wants to develop a financial plan for her retirement the following July. As her coach, we would make note of that and bring it up in the coaching conversations from time to time ("What are you thinking about that financial plan—are you ready to get started?"). If the client says, "No, not now," we assume she still wants it, even if she isn't making any progress toward that want. This is what many coach training programs refer to as "holding the client's agenda."

The life coach's job is to hold clients' wants and make sure they don't get lost. In other words, while clients are clarifying what they want, creating multiple pathways to get there, and going through the day-to-day action plans to accomplish their goals, the life coach supports, encourages, and reminds clients of what they said they wanted in all aspects of their lives (their agenda). At some point, a client may decide that a particular item is no longer something he really wants. Until he says so, the life coach continues to hold it as something the client said he wanted. The life coach helps clients define their mission, purpose, and goals and articulate their dreams, wants, and hopes to achieve the outcomes they desire.

You will be amazed at the scope of wants your life coaching clients identify. Just like your list from chapter three, our coaching clients have diverse wants. Clients tackle even the most difficult goal with anticipation and hopefulness because they understand the principle of possibility and the powerful, supportive nature of the life coaching relationship. Likewise, we know you won't have a problem with clients' *not* wanting to do the work. They go for their wants when they are ready.

## We Are Partners and Cocreators with Clients

Most coach training programs agree that the power in the life coaching relationship isn't in the coach or even solely in the client but in the relationship itself (Ellis, 1998; Leonard, 1998; Whitworth et al. 1998). Contrasted with therapy, where the therapist is seen as the expert, the client sets the tempo in the coaching relationship, and the coach collaborates with the client on goals. To collaborate in this way, the coach must get out of the way and relinquish the control to the client—a difficult task for some former therapists. The coach's role is to create an environment in which clients can fully focus on their wants, dreams, and desires, and the multitude of ways they can achieve them.

Because the relationship is mutually designed and both the coach and client are intimately involved in making it work, it has the power to nourish both the client and the coach. In fact, most life coaches report an exhilaration and energy associated with their work. Life coaching is sometimes challenging, yet it is common for us to leave a coaching session feeling happier, more fulfilled, and excited than when we began it. This is a pleasant change from traditional therapy sessions that could leave us exhausted and questioning whether anything positive was happening to forward the client's best interests.

Remember that the life coaching relationship is a dance. You will have wonderful partners (your clients) and a huge array of dance steps (their wants) to explore.

# PART III

# Powerful Transition Tools

# CHAPTER SEVEN

# Getting Started as a Life Coach

*Our beliefs about what we are and what we can be
precisely determine what we will be.*
—Anthony Robbins

We've learned that the strength of the life coaching relationship is mutually designed by both the coach and client for the sole benefit of the client's learning and achievement of his or her goals.

The life coaching dance requires you, the coach, to use your intuition, logic, great listening skills, sense of humor, and all of your caring support. It is important to remember that this is a partnered dance, not a solo performance. To keep the dance fluid and graceful, you must always be attentive to your clients' intentions and actions. As your clients' goals are achieved and their learning enhanced, changes may also occur in their life purposes and values. Your task is to remain flexible and to "dance in the moment" with each client. This approach both supports the client and provides a climate for greater learning.

Just as certain basic components are present in dancing (such as music, a dance floor, shoes, special clothing), basic components are also present in the life coaching relationship or dance. Let's look at some of the basics you'll need to set the context of your first formal coaching conversation.

## The Intake Session

You are familiar with the initial, scheduled appointment with a client, typically called an *intake*. In life coaching, intakes may take several forms and may vary in location and length, depending on the needs of the client and the coach. Intakes can take place in person or by telephone, and they are usually 1–2 hours long. You will need to be organized for intake appointments, have several documents prepared in advance, and know thoroughly the procedures you wish to cover in the session. Your intake session is another opportunity to enroll the client in the power of life coaching and provide a taste of the possibilities available through it. We highly recommend working with a mentor coach before you conduct your first intake session. Doing so gives you the chance to ask your questions and practice some of the language you'd like to use.

First, let's look at some of the standard documents a life coach will use in association with the initial interview.

## Welcome Packet

Life coaches often design a Welcome Packet for new clients. This packet includes any forms you will use in the intake, as well as anything else you would like to give to your client. Some coaches send the client a copy of the Welcome Packet to complete and return prior to the first session. In this case, the content of the first session largely consists of reviewing the information provided by the client. We have included a sample Welcome Packet in the back of this book.

## Life Coaching Agreement

We strongly recommend that you create a life coaching agreement before you start coaching. This form describes what you can expect from clients and what they can expect from you. Having this agreement is particularly important for therapists who are transitioning into life coaching, regardless of whether or not they choose to continue to practice therapy along with their life coaching business. Developing your life coaching agreement helps you, as the coach, clarify your role in the relationship, as well as your expectations for the client. It provides a valuable tool for introducing life coaching specifics to the client. In most cases, we send or give the client a copy of the form to review before the intake. Then, during the session, we can clarify the various aspects of our agreement and expectations for one another.

There are many variations of life coaching agreements. Most coaches would be happy to show you their forms. The following is a life coaching agreement similar to what we use in our businesses, but it is simply a sample for your reference. We cannot vouch for its legality in your particular situation, and we recommend that you develop your own agreement and have it reviewed by an attorney. Additionally, we recommend that you retain the original in your client's file and give a copy to the client. This is a good practice for all your written agreements with clients.

### Sample Life Coaching Agreement
(Your name)

(Your business name)

(Your address)

Prior to entering into a life coaching relationship, please read the following agreement carefully and indicate your understanding by signing below. If you have questions, consult your coach before signing.

1. I understand that life coaching is based around a relationship with a life coach that is designed to facilitate the establishment of long-range goals and short-term objectives and the achievement of those goals.
2. I understand that the role of the life coach is to assist me with improving the quality of my life.
3. I understand that life coaching is comprehensive in that it deals with almost all areas of my life, including work, finances, health, education, relationships, and spiritual issues. I acknowledge that deciding on how to handle these issues and implementing my decisions remains my exclusive responsibility.
4. I understand that life coaching is for people who are already basically successful, well adjusted, and emotionally healthy.
5. I understand that the confidentiality in the life coaching relationship is limited. Confidentiality will not apply to certain crimes that have either been committed or are planning to be committed. Such crimes may need to be reported to legal authorities. It is also possible that certain

topics discussed could be reviewed with other life coaching professionals for training and development purposes.

6. I understand that life coaching does not treat mental disorders as defined specifically in the *Diagnostic and Statistical Manual of Psychiatric Disorders*. If I have anything in my past indicating that I have an unresolved and serious emotional or physical problem or a mental disorder, I certify that I am not using life coaching as a substitute for assistance from a mental health professional or a medical doctor.

7. I will not use life coaching as a substitute for counseling, psychotherapy, psychoanalysis, mental health care, or substance abuse treatment.

8. If I am currently in therapy or under the care of a mental health professional, I will have consulted with that person regarding the advisability of my working with a life coach. Additionally, I will inform my coach of this relationship.

9. I will not use life coaching in lieu of professional medical advice, legal counsel, accounting assistance, business consultation, or spiritual guidance, and for each of these areas I understand I should consult the appropriate professionals. I acknowledge that I will not use life coaching as a substitute for such professional guidance. I further acknowledge that all decisions on dealing with these issues lie exclusively with me.

10. I agree to complete regular evaluations of the life coaching process and notify my coach immediately of any concerns.

Signature _____

Please print name _____

Date _____

Address _____

City_____ State _____ Zip _____

Coach's initials: _____

Copy given to client on: _____

## Intake Components

Along with the commonly used documents, there are some standard procedures or tasks you'll want to accomplish during your intake session. Depending on the time you allow for intake, you may not accomplish all of these. If not, we urge you to address them in the first couple of sessions. Although not an exhaustive list, we've included a sample of common intake components coaches wish to accomplish. We've also added some samples of language a life coach might use during these parts of the intake session.

1. *Collecting all relevant client directory information.* (You can include a request for this in your Welcome Packet or develop a form to use as you interview the client.) You will need the client's name, address (home, office), phone and fax numbers (home, office, cell), e-mail addresses, website information, name and contact information of administrative or personal assistant (if applicable), birthday, and names and contact information of immediate family members.

2. *Learning what the client wants from you as a coach (today and in the future).* Ask clients how they want you to function as their coach, how they envision you helping them. Clarify if they want you to "hold them accountable," "challenge them," and so forth. Coach: "I'd like you to think about our relationship and how you might like to be coached. I want to give you what you want. We have some options we can consider. Let me explain."

3. *Learning who the client is.* Find out about his or her personal values and life vision or purpose. Coach: "What would you say are some of your values? What really matters to you? What is your purpose in life? When you think ahead, do you have a vision of how you'd like your life to be (now and in the future)?"

4. *Reviewing what the life coaching relationship is and how it is similar or different from other relationships the client may have.* During this section of the interview, the coach helps the client understand what to expect in this unique relationship. It is always helpful to first ask the client what he or she knows about life coaching so you have an opportunity to understand his or her perspective and explain how you as a life coach like to work with a client. You distinguish among friendships, consulting, and therapy relationships so the client is clear on how life coaching differs from those.

   During this time we also discuss what the client can expect over the course of the coaching relationship (including ups, downs, plateaus, periods where everything moves very rapidly, and periods where he or she may feel "stuck" or in a slump). It is important to normalize these fluctuations for clients and to reassure them that you will be at their side through all these wonderful highs and possible lows.

5. *Teaching the client how he or she can best facilitate personal growth.* Client growth is facilitated by setting an agenda, telling the truth, completing homework, and "requesting."

We believe that life coaching relationships are most successful when coaches state clearly what they expect from the client. Letting clients know that they are in charge of (a) setting the agenda for each session, (b) telling the truth about what is going on with them and the coaching relationship (from their perspective), and (c) completing all homework is an important part of early intake discussions. Because the intake includes a large amount of content, we also recommend that you continue to follow up with your clients on these expectations over the next few sessions.

"Requesting" in the coaching relationship is an important tool, and teaching clients about the requesting process is a valuable lesson. It is a great way to help clients get what they say they want without leaving them feeling trapped or required to do something that isn't a fit for them. Coaches often make requests of clients, and clients need to understand that they have at least three possible responses.

For example, a coach might say, "Since you've said this is what you want, I request that you commit to a cardiovascular workout for at least 45 minutes next Monday, Wednesday, and Friday." The client has three options in response to this request. The client can agree with the request, "Yes, I will." The client can decline the request, "No, I won't." Or the client can propose a counteroffer, "Monday, Wednesday, and Friday won't work for me, but I'll agree to Monday, Wednesday, and Saturday."

6. *Discovering what is going on in the client's life right now.* Trained therapists are great at collecting this narrative. Clients usually love telling their stories. Clients will tell you their challenges, why they haven't created the life of their dreams, and who they blame, along with why they are proud of certain acts, relationships, or accomplishments in their lives. Take good notes, as this information provides a great springboard to begin moving the client into the future.

7. *Asking the client to identify goals, results, and personal development changes that he or she would like to work on in life coaching.* You will continue to collect this information throughout the coaching process. Your task as the coach is to begin helping the client focus on his or her wants in all areas of life so that both of you can look into the future and get a sense of where the client wants to go (today, tomorrow, next month, next year, next decade).

8. *Reviewing your life coaching agreement form and any special policies you have regarding your coaching practice.* We discussed this earlier in the chapter.

9. *Reviewing fee policy.* Collect payment for the intake and the first month of coaching, if you use that model.

10. *Requesting a favorite photo.* During our intake sessions we frequently ask clients to pick a favorite photo of themselves and give us a copy. We also discuss why this is a favorite and meaningful photo to them. Later in the coaching relationship, it is common for clients to send pictures of new babies, grandchildren, a new home, or even a clean desk or closet to share their lives with us or to report their progress in attaining their goals.

## Office Management and Fee Collection

### *Home versus Outside Office*

If you already have your own private therapy or counseling practice, you are familiar with office management and fee collection. You'll need to make decisions regarding whether to continue your therapy practice and add on a coaching niche, or to move completely into life coaching. There are varying opinions regarding the wisdom of maintaining two practices, and we suggest you visit with therapists who have made the transition to facilitate your decision. Beyond deciding if and how you will continue your therapy practice, many of the processes you have in place, such as filing systems, technology support, and billing procedures, will be transferable. We strongly recommend that if you maintain a therapy practice while working as a life coach, you develop separate documents for your life coaching practice and even consider a separate phone line. Be very clear with clients about your life coaching role and your therapist role in order to avoid confusion and help limit potential liability concerns.

If you are not currently self-employed as a helping professional with an independent office, you have options to consider, too. Whether to get an outside office or work at home is a central question for many new life coaches. For this decision, you will want to consider not only your finances and at-home resources, but also the type of practice you wish to have. For example, if you plan on meeting clients in person, having an outside office may make more sense. However, if you plan to do the bulk of your counseling on the phone, you can have a home office, live anywhere, and work in your pajamas if you want to. Both of us work at home and have been successful in defining our space and work schedule, so having a home office is a fit for us. We both maintain our practices when we travel unless we've negotiated and scheduled a "time out" with our clients in advance. Deb spends 6 months, spring through fall, in the mountains of Idaho and winters at her place in Maui. A home-office-based life coaching practice and the addition of a laptop computer make this mobile coaching lifestyle very feasible.

If you have never worked from a home office, it is important to consider potential distractions, such as children, pets, and noises during your calls and home chores that call you away from your office. Another challenge is the tendency to become isolated. Some individuals feel they need the discipline and structure that an outside office provides. We've known former therapists who go into partnership with another life coach and share an office space by coaching on alternate days. Similarly, a group of independent coaches could rent office space together. A coaching practice does not require a lot of space. A desk, chair(s), phone, computer system, and a fax machine are the basic office needs for most life coaches.

Numerous resources are available that provide sound advice on establishing a home-based business, so we won't go any further into the details. We've included some in the Resources at the end of the book. Before you make a unilateral decision for a home- or office-based practice, we encourage you to explore this topic by both consulting the literature and talking with folks who practice using both models.

## *Telephone Systems*

A telephone headset is the most essential piece of office equipment for any life coach who works on the phone. Clarity of sound and comfort are critical qualities of an effective headset. You must be able to hear your clients, and they you, without distortion. Depending on the size of practice you desire, you may spend five or more hours on the phone during a given day. Your headset must be comfortable. Cordless headsets provide the flexibility to move about, thus reducing the fatigue of being tied to your desk. Most office supply stores carry entry-level headsets, and many online sources exist as well. Talk to your coach about particular aspects he or she believes are important.

Your telephone coaching practice may function on one telephone line for a while, but once you have five to ten clients, you'll want to consider a second line (one for your business and one exclusively for client calls). As your practice grows, you may need a dedicated line for a fax or modem. Voice-mail or an answering machine on your business line is also essential. There are increasingly sophisticated office programs available for your computer that may provide solutions to your technology questions.

## *Fee Schedule Collection Methods*

We have seen a full spectrum of coaching fees and fee-collection methods during our years as life coaches. When you establish your coaching business (which we'll discuss in a later chapter), you'll need to ask yourself some important questions related to your fee schedule and collection methods. Here's a little exercise to get you started thinking.

---

### ☞ TRY IT! ☜

Ask yourself some of these questions now as you begin to think about your fee schedule and collection methods. Please record your responses in your journal.

1. How many times a month do I want to meet with each of my clients?
2. What is an ideal session length for me?

*continued on next page*

---

3. What holidays do I want to have free from work?
4. How will I accommodate client vacations, leaves of absence, or sabbaticals?
5. On what days or hours do I want to coach on a regular basis?
6. How much time, beyond my direct coaching time, do I want to spend on other business-related tasks, including preparation and review of sessions and responding to voice-mail messages and e-mails?
7. What specific income goals do I want to meet with my life coaching practice?

After reviewing your answers to these questions, draft a tentative "ideal" life coaching schedule and a fee-collection policy for yourself. Here's an example of one life coach's "ideal" schedule:

This particular life coach wanted only a part-time practice, with the rest of her schedule open for writing and family activities. She elected to coach three weeks out of the month, with the first week of each month free from coaching. Additionally, because she wanted structure in her schedule, she chose to coach only on Tuesdays and Thursdays. Clients who couldn't fit into that schedule were referred to other coaches. With regard to hours spent per month with clients, she felt that four hours was her minimum. Therefore, she elected to schedule 1½-half hour appointments with clients. She routinely scheduled a lunch and afternoon break into her Tuesdays and Thursdays. This schedule allowed her to have the ideal lifestyle she wanted, while still achieving a successful income stream.

An effective option for new life coaches is to elect to take a few clients for free or a greatly reduced fee while getting started. However, be certain to set a clear "introductory period" of free or reduced-fee service so that these clients do not expect this arrangement to continue indefinitely.

As far as collection methods go, you can collect at the time of appointment if you are coaching in person, but for most coaching relationships we recommend that you collect in advance for the upcoming month of coaching. This way, clients will have already paid and are invested in doing the work, even during a brief slump. Similarly, they are not voting on their coaching with their payment. In either case, you need to be very clear about your policies regarding "no shows" or client-cancelled appointments. It has been our experience that the more time you spend in advance thinking about how you would handle a variety of scenarios, the more likely you are to feel successful about your fee-collection policies.

If you do have a problem with fee collection, we encourage you to discuss what is going on with your client immediately and ask when you can expect payment. Your relationship is professional, and it is important that payment problems do not get in the way of your coaching. Significant problems are avoided if expectations are addressed in advance and clearly described in the client's materials. The best solution for most dilemmas, such as nonpayment, is simply to talk about it. If the problem continues after discussion with the client, seek some mentor coaching and consider your options. We rarely see this problem occur, and it seldom continues after such a discussion.

## Your Life Coaching Sessions

How you prepare for coaching sessions is a matter of individual choice. Over time, however, we believe that you will be a more effective life coach if you routinely schedule time into your calendar and prepare in advance for each of your coaching sessions. Here are some general suggestions for preparation before a coaching call:

1. Use a coaching preparation form.
2. Review your notes.
3. Create an agenda for the call.
4. Consciously "hold" your client as you prepare.

### Use a Coaching Preparation Form

One way to prepare for a coaching conversation is to have your client tell you what has happened since the last session, and what he or she wants from this session. The best way we have found to do this is through the use of a coaching preparation (prep) form. For us, the coaching prep form is a "must-have" coaching tool. A sample of this form follows. We strongly recommend that you orient all your clients to the prep form early in your coaching relationship; hold clients accountable for completing and returning the form prior to each coaching session. There are several advantages for both the coach and client to routinely use a prep form.

## Coaching Preparation Form

*Please complete this form and fax or e-mail it to me at least 24 hours before our session.*

Today's date: _____

Name:_____

Fax #: _____

Coach fax and e-mail: _____

1. What wins, celebrations, or accomplishments have occurred since our last conversation?

2. What challenges (difficulties, complaints, energy drainers) do you currently face in your life?

3. What, if anything, did you not get done that you intended to do?

4. What do you want from our session today?

5. Once the session is complete, please write down what you have learned and what you intend to do as a result of our life coaching session. Then e-mail or fax a copy to me.

The coaching prep form requires clients to focus on the upcoming coaching conversation, answer a series of questions, and then fax or e-mail the responses to the coach prior to the start of the session. This activity has several benefits. First, it requires minimal time but is critical to helping clients maintain their coaching time as a life priority and show up for the call prepared and focused. It is fine if they choose to have a different agenda for the call, but the time spent focusing and clarifying what they want is extremely valuable. Second, it gives the coach information, before the call, about clients' celebrations, what they want to work on, what challenges they are facing, and what they haven't done that they intended to do. This information sets the stage for the coaching dance to begin!

The final entry on the form is completed after the coaching session. It asks the client to reflect on what he or she learned from the session and intends to do as a result. Answering this question helps clients incorporate the wants, goals, and insights identified in the session into their current intentions and future actions. It also helps clients hold themselves accountable during the time between calls for what they said they wanted to accomplish. Typically clients fax or e-mail this response back to you.

We have used coaching prep forms for several years in our practices and are firmly convinced that they significantly enhance the quality of the life coaching session by helping clients stay focused on their goals and steadily moving toward their ideal future. The prep form also helps us, as life coaches, be better prepared for each of our client sessions. Different coaches develop different forms and have varying expectations about how far in advance of the session they'd like to receive them. You can ask coaches to share their forms with you as you begin to develop your own.

Once clients understand the benefits of using a coaching prep form, they are very responsible about completing it in advance of the session and report that it helps them to be better prepared. With both fax and e-mail options, many clients can submit their prep forms even when they are traveling. An occasional miss typically is not significant.

A few coaches have told us about clients who repeatedly ignore their conversations about, and requests for, the coaching prep form. In those instances, we advised the coach to consider if this issue is personally significant enough for them that it might warrant a referral of the client to another coach. More times than not, the client who is resistant to trying a new process, such as the coaching prep form, is also resistant to change in other areas.

Referral is an individual decision for a coach. For some of us, the coaching prep form is an important tool for providing the client with the level of services we want to offer. For others, it may not be as important. Above all, open conversations should be held with the client from the beginning about anything of this nature that concerns how you, the coach, do your job.

## Review Your Notes

We take notes during our sessions and recommend that you consider doing so, too. Effective notes help you account for the many wants that clients tell you they hope to achieve. They further allow you to recall the detail of clients' lives and their changing life goals and values as the coaching relationship advances. We recommend that you take down the clients' exact words so that you can share those with them. Additionally, we routinely offer to take notes for clients and then send photocopies of our notes or summarize key points in an e-mail follow-up to the conversation. This is particularly valuable to clients when they have produced a long list of brainstorming activities or detailed strategies for how they want to achieve a particular goal.

Some coaches keep less extensive notes than we do, but we suggest always trying to include in your notes (1) homework the client has agreed to do, (2) major events coming up for the client, and (3) any goals or daily habits the coach is helping the client track. On occasion, a coach might want to consider tape-recording a session, such as in the case of training others or a hand injury. If you do consider this option, we strongly recommend that you discuss it with the client in advance and specify (in writing) the purpose of the recording and who will have access to its content. Secure the client's written approval to record the session prior to taping. Additionally, prior to any tape-recording of sessions (in person or on the phone), you should consult state laws regarding this type of activity.

No matter the format you use, we encourage you to schedule time to review your records before each session and occasionally schedule a time to review the entire client file to assure yourself that you haven't lost your focus on the client's wants and dreams. Preparation is a key ingredient in a successful coaching relationship for both the life coach and the client.

## Create an Agenda for the Call

We suggest that you use the coaching preparation form to create an agenda for the session. Whereas the client is the leader and author of what occurs in a session, the coach is responsible for bringing forth the possibility of the time together. Preparing your own outline or agenda for the session is valuable on occasions when clients just don't know where they want to begin or are not focusing well due to external issues. In that situation we might say, "Sounds like you're stuck. I've reviewed your coaching preparation form for today and have some suggestions for where we might begin—would you like to hear those?"

If the client seems hesitant or at any time shares a different agenda, simply drop your agenda and follow the client's lead. Some coaches refer to this as "dancing in the moment." A sample agenda might look like this:

Call with Teri 6/20/06

Greetings and sharing

Debrief her board meeting last Tuesday (see notes on her prep form).

Ask about celebrations, successes, wins.

Consider teaching about agreement keeping.

Review homework—exercise a half hour three times this week? What next?

Ask her about her graduate school wants (notes from January 31st)—does she still want this and what could she do to begin?

Confirm next call date.

## Consciously "Hold" Your Client As You Prepare

Prior to a session, take out the photo of your client and have it near you as you prepare your agenda. This is especially valuable for telephone relationships in which you may never meet the client face-to-face. This approach takes some adjusting for helping professionals accustomed to working in person. Focusing on clients' pictures helps direct your attention and creative energies toward them and creates a bond. We believe we are more effective as coaches when we hold our clients near in thought and spirit as we prepare for our sessions. This is a powerful renewal of our commitment to clients' fulfillment and success.

## Other Basic Life Coaching Logistics

Beyond preparation before and after the session, here are a few other logistical recommendations.

### *Request That Clients Call You*

Most coaches who practice telecoaching prefer to have clients call them. This encourages clients to take responsibility for their coaching. Occasionally, when an agency or foundation pays us to coach their clients, we call the client and then bill the agency for the call along with other negotiated expenses. Some coaches have an 800-number phone line and ask clients to call them on that number. This is fine if you choose to work this way, but then you have to remember that you are still paying for the call and must calculate this expense into business expenses. It is important to have the discussion about who calls whom and who pays for what during the intake session so that there is no confusion. We go over this area when we discuss fees, but you can also put it in writing in your Welcome Packet.

### *Start on Time and End on Time*

Time management in a life coaching practice is every bit as critical as in a therapeutic practice. From the onset, be clear with clients that you will start sessions on time and conclude them on time. If a client is late for a scheduled appointment, call her immediately. Usually it is a simple oversight and you can request that she call you right back. We wouldn't bill a client for this brief call unless it became a habit. However, if clients are habitually late, we recommend that you discuss this with them as soon as it becomes apparent. Clients who show up late for coaching are often experiencing consequences of being late in other aspects of their lives or are just not being responsible.

Scheduling sessions back to back, with preparation time in-between for the next one, is a strategy some coaches use to manage their time. They know in advance that letting a session run too long will shorten preparation time for their next client. Dedicated and effective coaches will not let this happen.

## *Beyond the Session*

We often encourage clients to leave messages on our voice-mail or send us an e-mail if they need extra accountability or structure to pursue their goals. Clients sometimes call spontaneously with celebrations. If clients make requests between sessions by phone or e-mail, we try to accommodate their requests in our schedules (such as providing a clarification, sending an article we mentioned, or replying to a celebration). However, if a client developed a habitual pattern of always requesting extensive time between sessions, we would discuss this concern and attempt to reach a mutually satisfying outcome. Again, the best solution for most potential coaching relationship problems is early, frequent, and open dialogue and communication.

## *Liability Concerns*

We are not attorneys and do not profess to have any expertise in this area. As with most helping professions, it is wise to be aware of the potential liability associated with life coaching. Prevention of risk is the preferred approach to liability concerns, just as it is in therapy. We discuss liability in depth during our coach training program, but here are several commonsense approaches to possible liability concerns.

1. Practice full disclosure in the intake session and throughout the relationship repeatedly.
2. Execute a written life coaching agreement with the client and review it from time to time.
3. Attend immediately to any concerns either you or the client has.
4. Establish regular, written evaluation of the coaching relationship by the client and the coach.
5. Follow the ethical guidelines provided by the ICF (see the Resources). If you consider a dual practice as therapist and life coach, we recommend getting a mentor coach who has a similar business setup.
6. Continue your professional development in life coaching by enrolling in a coach training program.

7. Attend professional conferences and become involved with a peer group of life coaches.
8. Inquire, read, and ask questions about ethics and liability issues, particularly those related to national and state helping professional guidelines. Refer to state and national licensing boards, associations, and professional journals.
9. Regularly check in with clients regarding the relationship and their expectations.
10. Keep thorough notes.
11. Get a life coach yourself!
12. Consult a lawyer when necessary.

Now you know some key components that comprise the intake interview and regular life coaching sessions. Next we will examine specific tools that will support your transition into the exciting field of life coaching.

# CHAPTER EIGHT

# The Basic Life Coaching Model:
## *Skills and Strategies*

*Most conversations are just alternating monologues. The question is,
is there any real listening going on?*

—Leo Buscaglia

Coaching and therapy are both more than "just listening" to clients. Masterful coaches, just like masterful therapists, learn various skills, strategies, and techniques that become integrated over time and ingrained in their unique way of working with clients. In this chapter we examine the basic structure of the coaching relationship from a simple, yet extremely powerful, coaching model. We then offer additional skills and strategies that are useful tools for your coaching tool kit. As you read about these skills, you may be struck by how simple they seem at first glance. Learn these basics with a beginner's mind, and then begin using them with coaching clients. Eventually you will find that using these skills becomes second nature for you. They are also effective tools when you are stuck or are looking for a useful strategy to move a client forward.

## Initial Coaching Conversation

Coaching is best understood as a series of conversations aimed at evoking the best in your clients and helping them realize what they want to change, improve, or add to their personal or professional lives. The initial conversation can occur even before you are hired as a coach. Whenever someone expresses interest in experiencing coaching or interviewing you as a prospective coach, you can follow the model presented here, even if you have only a few minutes to demonstrate the power of coaching. In this way, you can shift to "coaching mode" rather than just have a conversation. Coaching actually becomes a way of being present with people. Remember, before you start to coach, you should seek the other person's permission by asking, "May I coach you?" or "May I offer some coaching to you?" For example, here is a very common and powerful way to allow someone to experience coaching when you only have a few minutes. You might meet someone at a party or at lunch, and, having already described what you do as a coach, it is very effective to provide him with an experience of a brief coaching interchange rather than describe it. Ask the person to describe a goal he wants to achieve—a big dream or something he wants to be different in any area of his life. This is not just problem solving; you can reframe the problem as an opportunity and shift the person's thinking about future possibilities and authentic desires in any area of his life. For example:

COACH: Well, Bill, you seem interested in what I do as a life coach. Would you like to experience how coaching might work for just a few minutes here?
BILL: Sure. Sounds interesting.
COACH: Tell me something you are struggling with in regard to living the life you really want. This might be a long-term goal or vision, a change you want to make in any area of your life, or something you are putting up with that you would like to change or complete.
BILL: Well, my biggest frustration is my inability to be more organized. I get overwhelmed with all the things I have to do in both my work and personal life.
COACH: Great. That is so common. So let me ask you, where or how do you feel the most disorganized?
BILL: I guess both with my time and with all the clutter in my office.
COACH: Do you see any way in which those might tie together?
BILL: What do you mean?
COACH: In coaching, our clients begin by "de-cluttering" their life—by getting rid of both physical and psychological clutter. Loose ends and things that are

out of place cause you to feel drained of energy. It is as if they pull you away from tasks or unfinished business. Does that make sense?

BILL: Yes! I don't even want to stay in my home office because it is so disorganized. I lose things and have piles of projects, and it just feels chaotic.

COACH: Got it! I have a request. This request is just something I would like you to consider. You can say no, amend my request, or agree to it fully. Okay?

BILL: Okay. I'm listening.

COACH: A disorganized physical space is often reflective of a disorganized mind, and that prevents you from focusing on moving toward what you really want in your business and in your life. So here is my request. I would like you to take a half-day this week to de-clutter your office. And I suspect you will need help. So I would like you to tell me who you think could agree to do that with you. Could you do that?

BILL: My wife tries to help me from time to time, but it is so overwhelming to her because she does not know where things should go or how to organize it to my liking.

COACH: Do you have a colleague or friend who might be helpful?

BILL: I would be too embarrassed to ask anyone or to allow anyone to see my office.

COACH: Okay. Here's the second part of my request. There are people in most towns called professional organizers. Look in the Yellow Pages or your Chamber of Commerce listing and find one. They usually do an initial free consultation and can give you a quick design for de-cluttering your office and keeping it more organized. They have seen it all, so there's no need to be embarrassed. Besides, I hired one too, and it really helped me not only work more efficiently but also reclaim energy that was being drained away from dealing with piles in my office or time wasted looking for stuff. Will you do that?

BILL: I will. Sounds as though I need it.

COACH: Great. Now, a big part of coaching is follow-up and follow-through, so even though you have not hired me, would you please call me or e-mail me and let me know when you will meet this organizer? I really want to know the outcome of your meeting, and I want you to have someone who really cares that this gets taken care of.

BILL: You got it. Thanks.

COACH: That is a quick example of how coaching works. Imagine having a partner you can contact on a regular basis to help you move on to even bigger goals and desires. The support and accountability are key and, as your coach, I stand for you. I really want you to get what you want in life and for all your possibilities and preferences to become realities.

Demonstrating coaching is the best way for potential clients to really get a sense of its power and value. Here, then, is our basic four-step coaching formula that is not only useful but also powerful as the default in all coaching conversations. (These skills are discussed in more detail later in the chapter.)

### Step 1: Listen and Clarify

The first question a coach might ask is, "What do you want?" or "What do you want to accomplish?" Whatever you ask initially should be simple and open-ended, to evoke a thoughtful response from the client. Listening soulfully to the client's responses sets the stage for deepening the coaching conversations yet to come. Dave Ellis (1998) describes *full listening* as "an invitation for people to discover their passion—a ticket into the client's soul and a magnet that draws out brilliance" and *soulful listening* as "the kind of listening where you're moved to the depth of your being by what another person says" (p. 33).

Here are some questions and guidelines for you to keep in mind as you listen to your clients' initial responses:

What do you hear?
What does the client need to hear herself say? Or think? Or wonder?
Reframe in order to give perspective and clarity to the client.
Ask evocative and powerful questions.

As the client speaks and answers the questions about her desires, hopes, dreams, and aspirations, you as the coach listen for things to clarify, magnify, examine more deeply, and validate for the client. In a live training, Ellis describes the coaching conversation as one in which the client has the unusual opportunity to say what she has never said, think what she has never thought, and be heard as she has never been heard.

## Step 2: Say What Is So

*Listen and reflect on what you are hearing.* An important aspect of coaching is "telling the truth," which means not stepping over anything that you hear, suspect, or want to amplify. Use your intuition and personal radar. Even if you are not totally accurate, the client will correct you and fill in the blank spaces. Telling the truth is not analyzing or guessing at causal events, as in therapy. It is simply letting the client know what you are hearing, at all levels of awareness, in her words, her energy, and her silence. Saying what is so includes both constructive and supportive comments. It can include areas of potential concern as well as overlooked strengths or opportunities to point out to the client.

*Listen for the gap.* The gap is the space between where the client is and where she wants to be. The majority of coaching occurs in the gap. Naming it, giving it structure and clarity, and identifying what lies beyond the gap are all part of the coaching.

*Focus on strengths.* Listen for the client's strengths, passion, and desire for change. Authentically endorse the positive. Do not make it up, but reflect back what you can actually support and acknowledge. One of the most powerful aspects of coaching is that someone actually notices our strengths, which others in our lives (including us) take for granted.

(*Note:* This is not the place to be confrontational or to point out obstacles in the client's path. The goal of early coaching conversations is to join with your client, determine if coaching is something that might benefit her, and determine whether she is the right client for you.)

## Step 3: Listen More

Once you have said what is so and clarified what you have heard, it is time to listen some more. Allow time here for the client to fully reflect on and respond to any "truths" you have shared and to expand or adapt her speaking. It is your role (as coach) to be curious, and to be a bit reflective about what you heard. By listening fully and responding truthfully and completely, (including sharing of intuitive responses) you invite the client to listen to herself as well. This opens the door widely for the client to see and experience the power of the coaching relationship and the coaching conversations that take place.

## Step 4: Request Action

Let's face it—the whole idea of being coached is to make some changes with the help of a coach. Consequently, the final step of every coaching conversation is to request action from the client. Make a request for a new behavior or way of being. Ask him to take a small step toward the changes he wants to make. For example, the man mentioned a few pages ago might be asked to clean up some of the clutter in his office. He might be asked to take three steps toward a larger goal or big dream that he has. Break it down into smaller steps and request that he tell you what he will do and when he will do it. This is the heart of coaching. Help the client to stretch himself to do what he has wanted to do but has not had the push to do it. Ask for new behavior—something creative and outside the box. The old way hasn't worked or he wouldn't be seeking coaching.

Remember that the best way to ask for action is to make a request, not to offer a suggestion or advice. Frame your request in such a way that clients can agree, disagree, or adapt what you are asking. That way, they own the action steps as theirs.

## Listening as a Coach

Listening as a coach is different from listening for pathology, history, pain, and psychological blocks. In life coaching, we *listen* to what clients are saying (and not saying), and we listen for unspoken wants, desires, passion, and possibilities. Remember, coaching is about designing the life and future that clients desire by listening for what it is that they want most.

A masterful coach listens for clients' visions, values, commitment, and purpose in their own words and intent. To *listen for* is to listen for the gap—an unrealized passion or an obstacle. The coach listens with keen attention and with purpose and focus that arise from the partnership that was designed individually with each client. The coach is listening for the client's agenda, not what the coach thinks the agenda or direction should be.

*Listening for the solution* is an obstacle to great coaching! This tendency blocks the powerful process of discovering and uncovering and the creative ideas that come from the coaching conversation. We natural helpers often jump to probable solutions that might work, but the power of coaching is in bringing out the best in our clients, not just giving possible solutions to them as a quick fix. In sports, athletic coaches do not just tell athletes what to do, they coach them to find the way that works for them, within tried-and-true methods of practice and training. Coaching does not involve advising or training. Either one of those elements can be part of the overall relationship, but each must be labeled as such and used at a minimum. In other words, clarify your role if you do something other than coaching.

In addition to *listening to* and *listening for* clients, great coaching also uses a type of listening that we call *listening with* clients. This is listening consciously and deeply from the heart to what is evoked in us by the client's words, energy, and being. Pay attention to the images, emotions, and sensations that resonate within you. These are sources of great wisdom and breakthroughs that are available to you and your clients.

Deep listening as a coach involves all three levels of listening described above and is significantly different from how we listen to a therapy patient or a truly mentally disturbed individual. Deep listening can also be powerful in everyday living with those whom we really care about.

---

### ☞ TRY IT! ☜

Try deep and soulful listening as a coach this week with three different people. Ask them for feedback on how you did.

Use the basic coaching formula with at least one person this week and notice how you did. Get feedback from that person as well. How was it different from therapy? What happened as a result of the action request? How did you feel as the coach?

---

## Telling the Truth as a Coach

The second step in the basic coaching formula is saying what is so, or telling the truth. In coaching parlance, this does not mean to confront, question the client's integrity, or make the client wrong. Telling the truth is about pointing out potential incongruencies or intuitions about problem areas as well as acknowledging and endorsing the client's strengths. As a coach, say what you mean—just don't say it mean!

In coaching, we focus on strengths and then create actions to create new strengths while building on those already present in the client's life. We make a distinction between complimenting, acknowledging, and endorsing. In fact, you might think of these on a continuum:

Complimenting ➡ ➡ ➡ ➡ ➡ Acknowledging ➡ ➡ ➡ ➡ ➡ Endorsing

The arrows imply that as you move from left to right, the coach's comments gain increased depth and specificity. *Complimenting* someone is a good habit to have—about what the client did, what she wore, how she looks, and so on. *Acknowledging* goes a bit further and includes comments about a client's specific behavior or way of being that shows up in something she did. When you acknowledge someone, you speak a little deeper about her being and the "who" more than the "what." *Endorsing* goes even further to include a deeper level of articulation than what goes into acknowledging; it includes intuitive comments about the heart of being. An endorsing comment is more about the "who" than the "what" of the person being endorsed. It is targeted more to *being* than doing or having.

A very powerful coaching skill is being able to authentically acknowledge or endorse qualities, actions, abilities, or gifts that clients exhibit as their stories unfold. The power is in the delivery of the truthful message about what you hear, see, or intuit as the coach that the client most likely rarely (if ever) hears about herself. Here is an example.

A client named Joan comes to you for coaching and wants to be able to grow her business in a way that is not as challenging and overwhelming as her current job. She feels unfocused, a little lacking in business acumen, and generally unsure if she is on the right track. She feels that her life is out of balance, with her business leaking into her personal and family time. After listening to the client's story and desires for several minutes, you as a coach might say something like this:

*Complimenting*: "Joan, I want to tell you that you are doing the right thing here. You are focusing on what really matters. Way to go!" (Complimenting is positive but too ordinary and shallow for powerful coaching.)

*Acknowledging*: "Joan, as I hear you share your dreams as well as your frustrations, I want to acknowledge you for having such a great vision and for being willing to seek help. You have big plans and you are smart not to try it alone." (Acknowledging both validates what the client is saying and who she is. It speaks to both doing and being.)

*Endorsing*: "Joan, I have to tell you how struck I am by how you reveal your vision. Listening to your words and feeling your passion really help me see and sense you as a very caring being who is up to big things. You have eloquence in your style that is unique and that expresses the joy and excitement in your life's purpose that you want others to experience in their lives. Thanks for letting me experience that part of you." (Endorsing is very close to acknowledging but goes deeper. A coach endorses by authentically commenting on the uniqueness of the client in reference to the current discussion of the goals. It is mostly about who the client is—the human being more than the human doing.)

## Action as the Goal of Coaching

As we stated earlier, action is the result that all clients want from coaching. Although there are action-oriented approaches to therapy, designing action plans with clients in coaching is a cocreative process that emerges from the coaching conversations, as opposed to psychotherapy, where the therapist often gives assignments or prescriptive suggestions.

Coaching is a way to assist your clients in charting their journeys. There is a saying, "You cannot change the wind . . . but you can adjust your sails." That is partly what we do as coaches. We help our clients make adjustments with planning, focus, and follow-through (action). As coaches, we do not design the course for our clients. They may create and design their futures with our action requests or suggested experiments. We really lead from behind. However, we might be familiar with clients who express resistance to action and who move from one issue to the next to avoid making the necessary changes in their lives. If you have a client like that in coaching, you will want to explain that the process of coaching is to assist him in defining his vision and clarifying his goals to make his life as fulfilling as possible. If you have clients who are unable to improve their focus and action in coaching, they may not be coachable (yet) and they might need an appropriate referral to a therapist to help with the resistance. Coaching may be something they can return to at a later date.

Coaches work with clients on long-term vision as well as short-term actions for the next week, the next day, or even the next hour. People tend to get stuck in the future or the past. The purpose of action requests in coaching is to help clients carry out actions in the present that will make them more likely to achieve their desired future. As coaches, we help our clients design a future path, but we also create actions for living in the present. The magic of effective coaching lies in the ongoing relationship, but the outcomes come from built-in accountability to the coach. The key coaching questions toward the end of any coaching call or session are, "What will you do? By when? And how will I know?" This format creates accountability for the client that requires her to be purposeful and active before the next coaching conversation.

Action requests in coaching are often balanced between *doing* and *being*. Clients want to do something differently in their life or work, and they often forget the "who" and focus more on the "what." Carl Jung said, "Your vision will become clear only when you can look into your own heart. Who looks outside, dreams. Who looks inside, awakens" (1933, p. 57).

# ≺ CHAPTER NINE ≻

# Advanced Coaching Skills

*Excellence demands that you be better than yourself.*
—Ted Engstrom

Learning lots of skills and techniques in coaching is similar to learning the skills involved in driving a car. You will very likely be conscious of using them, and even somewhat structured at times when trying to use them. However, eventually you will forget the details and just coach. All the while these skills become integrated into your coaching style, they are always available as references or reminders when you feel you need more structure or strategy. We find it useful to have lots of coaching tools to help us stay flexible and not get stuck in a few default methods. Trying new tools keeps our coaching fresh and exciting. We believe that what really guides clients and their progress toward the life of their dreams is the coaching process, not the coach!

Coaching is more than just applying the principles and practices of solution-focused counseling to a coaching client, although many of those techniques and questions can be helpful. Coaching is much more than solving problems or eliminating barriers, although clients may seek coaching for either of these reasons. As we have stated, life coaching is about creating the life one really wants to live. It goes beyond problem solving and into life design and fulfillment. As problems are resolved and barriers reduced or removed, clients move closer to their goals. Being free of these former obstacles allows and encourages coaching clients to feel empowered—energized and *on purpose* for what they want to change in their life—and therefore able to discover ways to realize their intentions.

## Skills and Tools for Empowering Clients

In Chapter 8 we discussed the importance of listening for strengths and acknowledging or endorsing the client. This material should be reviewed, as these skills are the basis for empowering clients. First, be clear with clients about the existing strengths or gifts they already present; second, build on those strengths and gifts; third, in your coaching, choose any or all of the following skills for empowering clients:

Being curious
Standing for
Reframing
Never making the client wrong
Preferencing
Using possibility thinking
Using powerful questioning
Using purposeful inquiry
Using a compassionate edge
Using metaphors, stories, and analogies

Let's examine each of these.

### *Being Curious*

One of the unique characteristics of a great coach is to be curious with clients. Being curious implies a level of detachment from the outcomes, which allows the coach to listen to what clients say they want and what they say gets in their way. This stance helps clients experience a nonjudgmental space in relation to what they want to undo or decrease, what they want to do more of or increase, and how they want to be different as a person. Using curiosity as a coach helps take you out of the expert role and join in your clients' adventures of discovering what it is they really want, before the temptation to find solutions or actions arises in you too quickly. This is empowering because a client's response to your curiosity very often leads to his or her own self-discovery. We all have experienced feeling more charged up when we have discovered our own answers or direction. Curiosity helps the coach stay out of the way and assist the client to uncover or discover his or her own brilliant answers and solutions. Coaches take a powerful stance when they hold the perspective that clients have the answers to their concerns and challenges within them. The coaching relationship (or process) is designed to facilitate the discovery of those answers.

*Example*: The coach might say, "Mary, I am curious about your desire here. What is it that compels you to seek this goal? How will your life be better when you achieve this goal?" Curiosity is a mindset that allows the coach to ask powerful or evocative questions in a nonjudgmental and inquisitive context.

### Standing For

Many of the coaching skills presented here are ways to empower clients by validating and acknowledging a part of their being or specific behaviors. "Standing for" emphasizes *what* the client wants in her life rather than *who* she needs to be to get it. As a coach, you *stand for* clients' dreams and desires simply by remembering them for clients and believing in the possibility of their realizing them. Who else in a person's life does that on a consistent basis? You remind clients of what they said they wanted, and you remind them of their deepest desires, even when (or especially when) they get distracted. As the coach, you serve as a container for your clients' visions and the goals and objectives needed to achieve the change they really want. In the coaching relationship, you stand for clients and their wants even if those wants do not resonate with you or if you are not sure the client can achieve them. Unless clients' desires border on the unethical or illegal, you must suspend judgment and stand for the possibility and passion clients have for their goals. After all, we all know stories of great achievements accomplished when others thought they were unattainable because someone took a stand for what he or she believed was possible.

*Standing for* is a skill that shows up more in the way you relate to the client and in the sacred space you create in the coaching conversations, rather than being a technique or tool that you learn how to use. *Example*: A coach might respond to a client's big dreams and aspirations in this way: "Pete, I want you to know that I hold your dreams for you in our relationship. We may, from time to time, focus on more short-term or even immediate outcomes, but I stand for your larger goals, which are the crucible in which all these smaller accomplishments rest."

## Reframing

Reframing is a skill with which most modern therapists are familiar, and it is an equally useful skill in coaching. In reframing, you find other words or descriptors for something that appears to be a challenge, problem, or deficiency in the client's view. You place the behavior or perception, as articulated by the client, in a new context or frame. This new frame allows the client to see the situation or concern in a new way. Rather than viewing the problem as a weakness, it can be seen as an opportunity for learning.

*Example*: The client says, "I get so distracted from my goals much of the time. I sit down to write my workbook for my seminars and schedule more presentations, but I just get stuck and go nowhere."

The coach replies, "It seems to me that you are really the visionary and leader in your trainings. You are not the person to work with the details. What if you find someone to take on the details of the planning, scheduling of the seminars, and finding a cowriter for the workbook? Your strengths are in the inspiration and delivery of the material, not in the perspiration and the details of the scheduling and planning."

Great teachers and mentors have always used reframing or "metaview" in their teaching. In the movie *Dead Poets Society*, Robin Williams, a prep school poetry teacher, uses reframing masterfully. He asks his class to come up, one by one, to the front of the room and stand on his desk in order to give them a different view of the classroom. That is a visual description of what reframing does with coaching clients. As coaches, we ask clients to look at their dilemma with a different frame around it—to look at it from the future they want or to view it from a "metaposition," as if they are above themselves, looking at themselves. Practice using reframing with your clients and notice how often and naturally you begin to use it as a method for helping them change their perceptions. Please note that this is not just "sugar coating" a negative situation—it puts the situation in a new framework, which then allows and encourages clients to seek different action choices based on revised perceptions.

## *Never Making the Client Wrong*

Never making the client wrong may be the most difficult skill in coaching. We, as humans, are so familiar with finding fault or correcting others' mistakes, especially if we think we know the truth or right answer. As a coach, you are hired to evoke the client's brilliance, which implies that he *is* brilliant but may not fully express that brilliance in his life. When a client does not follow through on an assignment or stick to commitments, the coach needs to examine and speak with him about that behavior. However, the key skill here is to conduct the discussion in such a way that the client still feels supported even while having a conversation about something he did not do.

*Example*: A common occurrence in coaching is for the client to have failed to fulfill the commitments and achieve the goals to which she agreed in the last session. As coaches, we might respond in this way: "Cecilia, I hear that you did not complete the tasks you set out to do this week. What got in the way and how can we discover together some new strategies for your success with this today? Or maybe we need to change the goals. What do you think? I really want you to have success with the changes and accomplishments you seek."

It is very important for the coach to focus on what clients want and not what the coach may think they need. If clients do not have a clear picture of what they want to be different in their lives, that is where the coaching begins—to discover that clear picture. You can remind clients of their objectives and desires and ask how you can best coach them to do what it is they want to do—*and not make them wrong in the process*. After all, whatever happens is just results, not failure, and results can be examined as learning opportunities. As coaches, we can point out what did not happen that clients said they desired and ask if they want to recommit. We can inquire about what got in the way or explore a new direction that clients may want to pursue. All of this can be done in a neutral and very caring way, without making clients feel wrong or like failures. There is probably enough of that in their lives already! Accept clients for who they are, where they are, what they do, and how they show up while helping them discover ways they can change behaviors, habits, relationships, or actions. Never making the client wrong is a precious gift we give our clients through the unique coaching relationship.

## *Preferencing*

Clients often come to coaching with a long list of things they think they should be doing, ought to have, or need to change. These "shoulds" are usually beliefs they have developed from the influence of other people, books, talk shows, and experts. Remember, coaching starts with the question "What do *you* want?" and keeps at that question until clients have broken through the list of shoulds and oughts and reached their needs and wants. Using the skill of preferencing, the coach encourages clients to look at their various desires for change and to articulate which they would prefer without initially providing any particular rationale. Preferencing helps clients increase their awareness of how they have been limiting themselves unconsciously.

The use of preferencing in coaching is simply a linguistic shift that allows clients to be less attached to the outcome. For example, the coach might say to a client, "Stephen, I see how upset you get when the meetings with your team do not go as you intended and surprises occur that seem to throw you off track. I would request that you have a preference for the outcome you would like and move toward that, possibly even stating it out loud. I would suggest that this might free you up to "go with the flow" of the meeting and not be distracted if your preferred outcome changes or is amended. Could you try that this week?"

A conversation that both of us often have with our coaching clients is about making distinctions. Clients can get too attached to big dreams. The skill of preferencing helps clients desire these dreams but also realize that these dreams are only their preference. We cannot predict the future. Although it is very wise to plan and to chart a course toward a destination, things happen that can knock us off course. So, coaching clients to understand the distinction between a *preference* and a *need* is crucial.

One of Pat's favorite quotes, which has been a compass in his life, is from *Notes to Myself* (1970) by Hugh Prather:

If everything were to turn out just like I would want it to, just like I would plan for it to, then I would never experience anything new: my life would be an endless repetition of stale successes.

In their wonderful book *Recreating Brief Therapy: Preferences and Possibilities* (2000), John Walter and Jane Peller state that they now work from a position of wonder and curiosity. They function more as personal consultants to their clients to help them discern how they would prefer to live their lives and to explore the possibilities. They even go so far as to suggest to helping professionals that the field "replace therapy with personal consultation or some other equivalent term" (p. 15). Sounds like coaching to us!

## *Using Possibility Thinking*

A powerful part of a coach's job is to be a possibility thinker with clients. As a coach, you partner with your clients in seeking possible solutions or new strategies to help them make the changes they want in their lives. Bill O'Hanlon (1999a), a therapist and writer whom we both admire, developed an approach to therapy he calls possibility therapy—a humorous and passionate approach to action-oriented therapy. This approach could be a variation on the old technique of brainstorming, but in coaching it is different in that the process is co-engineered by client and coach. When clients are stuck in a habitual way of thinking or a problem-focused orientation, possibility thinking encourages them to consider alternative ways of looking at their perceived problem or dilemma. Possibility thinking offers clients a method by which to suspend their current belief system and to explore a much larger field of potential choices. This technique may also work concurrently with the use of powerful, open-ended questions such as "What if . . . ?" or "What would it be like if . . . ?", which lead clients to view their possible futures in terms of different actions and expectations. Possibility thinking can also be encouraged in a light-spirited manner that we believe helps take the emotional attachment and seriousness out of clients' current views of their situations. Part of the real joy and excitement that comes from coaching is the process of challenging our self-imposed limits. Possibility thinking as a coaching skill is well received, fun to use, and often transformational for the client.

*Example*: The client might say, "I am so frustrated with my computer. It keeps freezing up, and the e-mail server loses outgoing mail. I don't know what to do. I hate technology!"

The coach could respond, "Marcia, I know this is frustrating. Let's brainstorm together some possibilities to remedy this, okay? Why don't you start with two or three things?" (*Note*: As a coach, we first encourage the client to think of a couple of possibilities. Then we might suggest a couple of others and try to come up with a list of eight to ten possible solutions, which often include some crazy ones such as, "You could take your computer out back and smash it with a hammer"). The point here is to get the client to think of strategies she has not thought of and to stretch into new possibilities. As the coach, we would use language such as, "This is just my best thinking here in the moment. I don't know if this would work or not, but what if you hired a computer tutor to come to your house each week?"

## Using Powerful Questioning

Most therapists are very familiar with the use of questions to evoke information from clients or perhaps to lead to new patterns of thinking about how their difficulties might be transcended or resolved. Solution-focused therapy, Ericksonian hypnotherapy, and NLP all teach methods that include the use of powerful questions. For example: "Suppose one night, while you were asleep, there was a miracle and this problem was solved. How would you know? What would be different?" (de Shazer, 1988, p. 118; see also Berg, 2005, pp. 59–61). Steve de Shazer and the Milwaukee Brief Therapy Institute became known for their miracle question, which is actually an evolution of the "big question" taught in Adlerian psychology (Adler, 1998).

Frankly, we believe that we could insert the word *coaching* in much of the work of de Shazer and his associates and make all of their theories applicable to this new paradigm of possibility. However, it is important to keep in mind that although many of the techniques of solution-focused therapy, and even Ericksonian or NLP approaches, could be applied in coaching, that does not necessarily mean that coaching is the paradigm. Simply working from a stance of possibility does not make what you do coaching. Though de Shazer, O'Hanlon, and others share similar posturing as coaches, other aspects of their practices are distinctly for therapeutic issues and not coaching issues. Coaching skills can be used with therapy clients, but that does not turn the therapy into a coaching session. Coaching is a cocreative relationship, whereas therapy is based on a client–expert hierarchy.

Powerful questions in coaching are meant to stimulate clients' thinking. These are questions to which the coach usually does not have the answer. They are meant to encourage the exploration of information and possible behavioral choices available to the client. In coaching, these questions are meant to expand both client's and coach's curiosity and wonder while keeping their own agendas in the background as much as possible.

Examples of powerful and evocative questions include the following:

"If you had all the money you needed, what would you be doing?"

"If you only had one month to live, what would you do differently?"

"What would be different in your life if, 1 year from today, your life was exactly like you would like it to be?"

"How would you know when you have gotten what you want?"

"If you did know, what might your response be?" (when a client is unclear as to what he or she wants).

A client might say, "I want to increase my sales and yet not have the business overwhelm my family and personal time." The coach might reply, "What would an ideal week look like for you if you had plenty of work time and your desired family and personal time?" Or, "How would you know when you had a good balance between work and personal life?" A powerful question evokes deeper thought from the client, and because it is a question to which the coach does not know the answer, it allows both the coach and client to explore possibilities and new ways of being or doing.

As you practice, you will not need to rely on this list but will become proficient in creating your own questions spontaneously during conversations with clients.

### Using Purposeful Inquiry

Using purposeful inquiry means asking questions for which you want an answer only later, after the client has used the question to focus her thinking. For example, we might have a client who is very driven to make a career transition to a new job or an entrepreneurial venture that would be more "satisfying." We would request that this client consider the following inquiry for the week between our sessions: "What would the components of a more satisfying life or career be?" We tell the client not to answer that question now, in the session, but instead to use it as an inquiry and to write down all her thoughts about it during the week. This type of question often leads to powerful insights and information that can catapult the client into exciting life changes. Purposeful inquiry might be compared to the Socratic method, where an in-depth examination is facilitated by staying focused on questions instead of looking for immediate answers. Socrates said, "A life unexamined is a life not worth living." Most of the time, the inquiries are the same as the powerful questions mentioned in the previous technique, but the purpose of these inquiries is delayed, in-depth thinking rather than answers on the spur of the moment. You, as the coach, can create these inquiries spontaneously toward the end of the call (or session), or you can have several standard inquiries that you compile and choose from as you see fit. Either way, inquiries can lead to incredible shifts in clients' thinking and can contribute to very stimulating coaching conversations. Purposeful inquiry is a coaching technique that is both fun and illuminating. Bear in mind what the poet Rainer Maria Rilke (1904) had to say about the value of questions:

> Be patient toward all that is unsolved in your heart. Try to love the questions themselves. Do not now seek the answers which cannot be given. Because you would not be able to live them. And the point is to live everything. Live the questions now. Perhaps you will gradually, without noticing, live along some distant day into the answers. (p. 27)

Purposeful inquiry is often the same kind of question as a powerful question, but is posited to the client with a request to contemplate it between sessions. It is not to be answered in the moment, but used as a question to think about, talk about, write about, and come back with the results of the inquiry. For example, the client might say, "I really feel frustrated in my career, like I am stuck in quicksand and not able to move." The coach would then respond, "I would like to give you a purposeful inquiry this week, okay? What would be different if you got out of the quicksand? Don't respond now. Instead, use this inquiry this week and report back to me. At the next session tell me what thoughts, images, or feelings you had about this exercise."

### Using a Compassionate Edge

Sometimes a coach needs to be truthful in a way that might appear confrontational. We like to think that difficult messages can be delivered in the coaching relationship with a compassionate edge, or what we call "carefrontation." When would you use the compassionate edge? We have used it to remind clients of our personal or professional boundaries. Although it does not happen very often in coaching, a client might overstep your availability and call for long conversations between scheduled appointments. A client also might send you lengthy marketing plans or business forms that you have not agreed to review as part of your coaching agreement. If you feel overwhelmed or sense that your time and coaching services are being overused, you need to bring up this matter with your client. You might also use the compassionate edge when clients engage in repetitive, unhealthy behaviors that block their success. Using the compassionate edge means that you can be truthful without being mean or nasty. *Compassion* means you give the information in a sensitive way, and edge implies that it might be blunt or "right to the point." You model good coaching for clients with this skill, and you also teach them a useful assertiveness skill they can use in their own life. If you tell a client, up front, that there might be a time when you need to be direct but that your intention is never to be hurtful or uncaring, it is well received when you deliver it.

For example, you might say, "I have something I need to say, and I need to be direct. I am going to say it with compassion because I do not want you to misconstrue it. However, if I don't say it well, I will clean it up." (The coach continues the conversation until the client is clear about the intent of the message.)

By prefacing your message with this statement, the client, with whom you have already built good rapport and trust, will be clear about your intentions when you deliver the message. The conversation can then continue in an open manner until the communication is clear and resolved of conflict. This skill, which takes practice, is crucial to successful coaching. For any of you who are college basketball fans, we like to say humorously that this skill is not from the Bobby Knight school of coaching (University of Indiana and Texas Tech University), but more from the Roy Williams school of coaching (University of Kansas and University of North Carolina). Knight had a confrontational, in-your-face style, whereas Williams used patient teaching to evoke excellence from his players. As coaches, we hope to rarely need to get in our clients' faces, but it's important to be able to do so if needed, without disrupting the trust we've developed with them. Keeping compassion front and center as we deliver our message allows us to speak the truth as we see it while preserving the relationship and honoring the bond between coach and client.

Can you think of a time when you might use a compassionate edge? Can you remember a time when someone else used it (or could have) with you?

Masterful coaches get quicker and more powerful results because of their willingness and comfort in using the compassionate edge. The use of this skill comes from the coach's unwillingness to tolerate mediocrity and insistence on continuing to be compassionate and empathic with the client. Clients expect coaches to guide them to excellence; using this skill can help because it moves clients to acknowledge unspoken truths, behaviors, or habits, and, as a consequence, to transform them into more purposeful actions.

Mastery of the compassionate edge has benefits for the coach as well. Once you become skilled and comfortable with it, you will find that you will attract high-powered clients who expect this edge from their coach. They are not just learning the skill; they haven't hired a coach to take baby steps or stay in their comfort zone; they are high achievers.

For example, a client might say, "I sent out ten letters this week and had two conversations with people about my new business." The coach might respond: "Jim, I really want for you to have the success you seek. You've set the bar too low. I would request that you commit to sending out one hundred letters this week and having two conversations a day describing your new business. You have to stop being a secret, and I want to raise the bar higher for you. Will you accept this challenge?" This is an "edgy" and aggressive approach by the coach, but it's used when the challenge can be done compassionately and can nudge the client to greater action.

### Use of Metaphors, Stories, and Analogies

Many therapists already use these techniques in their approach to psychotherapy. Whether these are natural for you or whether you need to learn how to use them better, metaphors, stories, and analogies are powerful tools.

METAPHORS

Dictionaries define a *metaphor* as a figure of speech in which a word or phrase denoting one kind of object or idea is used in place of another to suggest a likeness or analogy between them, as in "drowning in money." Metaphors provide the magic of a visual and creative use of words that stimulate new thought. At a conscious level, the client has a highly personal and bonded experience of the coach's understanding. At a deeper level, the message can bypass the client's awareness and go directly to his unconscious—the seat of 95% of perception and emotion, and the generator of behavior.

Metaphor making goes on effortlessly all the time—in country songs, on playgrounds, in your own household. Start to be aware of the metaphors you use naturally and the ones you hear used around you. Collect and treasure metaphors; listen for new, surprising ones and for whatever vibrates your "tuning fork." Here are some examples used in coaching situations.

1. Your client is a distracted businessman who wants to use his time more wisely and have energy for work as well as his personal life. In getting to know him, you learn that he plays blues guitar for his own pleasure. Remind him that if he practices time management skills one step at a time, eventually he will use them automatically, like making a C-chord effortlessly on the frets without thinking, and he will experience harmony between work and home.

2. Your client has a passion for woodworking. He tells you how stressed he's been, trying to get a project finished in time for his wife's birthday, and he knows that he makes mistakes when he hurries. You say, "Charlie, how can you tell when the top of that cabinet is level?" He describes using a carpenter's level. You answer, "So, Charlie, what can you do to ease up and get your own personal bubble to settle down right between those lines?"

3. Your client is a Wonder Woman executive who has a hard time slowing down but desperately wants balance in her life. You suggest that she spend time on the weekend in "canoe mode," just trailing her fingers in the water and letting life take her where it will for the day.

What do these examples have in common? They establish rapport and offer an embedded, implied suggestion. Roz Van Meter, a coach and graduate of ILCT says, "I had a hyperactive telecoaching client who kept speaking in such staccato rhythms that I had trouble focusing on his session. I asked him what kind of music his brain was playing. 'Well, some kind of salsa, I guess.' I asked him to take a long, slow breath and change to an easy-listening station. He took a deep breath and calmed down. His voice fell half an octave in pitch and slowed, we reconnected, and he was focused again" (personal communication, October, 2000).

Metaphors, analogies, parables, and allegories can be woven into a tapestry as elegant as a magician's cloak and as powerful as his wand. An experienced coach or therapist can:

- Listen for the client's own metaphors to tell you who she is.
- Match her world with parallel metaphors to let her know you understand.
- Use metaphors to confirm her desires and goals (what).
- Construct allegories linking where she is to where she wants to go.
- Create parables and dream weaving to create the map (how).

Stories—legends, myths, and epic ballads—have been the teaching method of transcended masters from Aesop's fables to Greek tragedies to the Bible to Sufi stories and family stories. Once you truly understand what the client wants and what stands in her way, you can become a storyteller, too. Start with "You know, I once knew a man who . . ." or "My Aunt Irma used to tell us about . . ." and construct a parable that parallels the client's dilemma and offers a solution—remember, not an exact match, but a parallel one.

Many of us may have learned to hone our skill in using metaphors, stories, and analogies by reading of the magic of Milton Erickson and his followers (Bandler & Grindler, 1975; Haley,1988, 1986; O'Hanlon & Martin, 1992; Zeig, 1994). Erickson's wizardry can be applied powerfully to coaching. After all, he was more of a life coach than a psychotherapist.

STORIES

Some coaches are skillful storytellers who are able to relate a true story or create one that teaches a point to be explored in coaching. Coaching stories are like those in *Chicken Soup for the Soul* (Canfield & Hansen, 1993); they are heartwarming, inspirational, and have a moral or point that relates to the client's situation.

### ANALOGIES

Like metaphors and stories, analogies can give clients a different perspective on their situation and create new ways to behave, think, and act in support of their goals. For example, a client might say, "I keep getting off track with my goals due to distractions, interruptions, and other things that happen during the week."

The coach could respond, "That is so very normal. What if you saw your life as a journey down a river on a rubber raft? You would naturally come upon some boulders and other obstacles along your journey. But if you are rafting, you would have a helmet, life preserver, and probably even a guide to help you navigate around or over some of the boulders. We all have boulders in our daily lives, and they are just part of the journey. How can you begin to find the support you need to avoid certain obstacles or make sure you have the right equipment and assistance if needed to navigate the others?"

The skills and techniques presented in this chapter are varied and in some cases may blend together. It's like having various types and sizes of tools in a toolbox. Some are hand tools, some are power tools, and some might be turbopowered. You might need all of them or just one or two. These skills can be practiced during your transition from therapist or counselor to coach. After using these skills purposefully for a while, they will become second nature for you. But if you ever feel "rusty" or just want to try something different with a client, refer to these as you would a recipe book. Adapt them to your heart's content and have fun as you help your clients step into the life they really, really want.

# CHAPTER TEN

# Developing and Marketing Your Life Coaching Practice

*If not now, when?*
—The Talmud

As therapists, we certainly were not taught much about building our business. In fact, we do not even call it a business—we call it a practice! Further, most of us were taught that it was even unethical and unprofessional to market or advertise our services. It was not until the late 1980s that we started to have Yellow Pages ads with descriptions of our services, and you certainly never mentioned in conversations at cocktail parties that you could help someone with his or her problem. As a coach you are a businessperson providing a unique form of assistance. You can speak about it, advertise it, and enthusiastically let people know you might be able to help them reach their goals. You can even meet in public to discuss how your services might be of use.

Obviously, a crucial component for your transition to coaching is learning entrepreneurial skills and some simple but powerful development and marketing steps for a successful business. It's only natural for most helping professionals to be uncomfortable with the idea of marketing or selling. In this chapter we show you new ways to approach marketing as a way of letting people know what you do.

## Marketing versus Selling

Most of us often confuse marketing with selling. We probably hear ourselves saying things such as:

"I don't like selling."

"I can't take rejection."

"Selling is unprofessional."

"I do not want to appear pushy."

"I became a therapist, not a salesperson."

We understand these fears. They come from your inner gremlin or your self-critic. But you have many options for marketing your business, and it can even be enjoyable and natural. Think of it this way. If you are right-handed and lost the use of your right hand, you eventually would become proficient and comfortable using your left hand. It just takes practice and a willingness to change. And this is a wonderful new opportunity for learning and repackaging your current skills.

We also believe that the marketing methods you use should be enjoyable (although they may take some practice to achieve a good comfort level). Remember that you are not knocking on doors or telemarketing to sell a product that people do not want. Most people will want coaching. The goal is to attract the type of client *you* want to work with and for whom your services are both valuable and affordable. Isn't that true for the professional services you utilize?

## Stop Being a Secret!

Our basic philosophy is that if you want people to hire you as a coach, you must stop being a secret. The principle of attracting clients is more powerful than the manipulative promotion and selling other sales professionals use, but if you are going to follow the principle of attraction, remember that the word action comprises more than half of the word. You will not get clients by just wishing and hoping that they would contact you. They need to know that you exist, what it is you do, and the benefits they (or those they might refer) will receive by working with you as a coach.

As we have trained helping professionals to become coaches, we have heard many people voice their beliefs, myths, and misconceptions about marketing. Our training approach is based on five key principles:

1. *Marketing is not selling.* We wish we had thought of it first, but as Peter Drucker, the business and management consultant, said so eloquently: "The purpose of marketing is to make selling unnecessary" (1974, p. 27). We definitely agree. Of course, technically, you *are* selling. You are selling your self and your service, but it should be done in a way that does not feel or look like stereotypical high-pressure selling. There is nothing inherently wrong with selling. We all sell and we all buy. Many of us, though, are uncomfortable with some types of selling that pressure people into buying something they did not want. Marketing coaching services simply involves opening a relationship and offering the possibility that coaching could greatly benefit the potential client. It is not meant to be manipulative, seductive, or dishonest. You will need to learn to market yourself until your business grows to the point of being filled mostly by referrals—the ideal position for a self-sustaining business.

2. *Therapists have the necessary marketing skills because we are trained to listen well and communicate clearly, and because we are good at creating relationships.* This is why marketing gurus of today, especially in service-oriented businesses, say that networking is the key to business success. What is networking? It is developing relationships with people so that they know what you do and you know what they do. Networking is the way business is built through cross-referrals or as a way of serving your clients. Coaches who become master networkers and who can refer their clients to other professionals or services that could address specific concerns will have a thriving business and a reputation as someone who knows whom to call or where to go. C. J. Hayden (1999) says, "Marketing is telling people what you do . . . over and over" (p. 5). So, the keys to success as a new coach come from figuring out what you want to say about your coaching, how to say it, and to whom you want to say it. If you really love what you do, people will experience your authenticity; even if they don't want to hire you as a coach, they may know someone who will. In coaching, you are hired more for who you are than for the specifics of what you do. If you are enjoying your life and you coach people so that they can, too, you are your own best advertisement. People want some of what you have. They will want you to help them achieve

the level of happiness and clarity of vision that you have achieved. All you need to do is guide them to develop their life according to their desired agenda.

3. *Marketing your practice successfully and easily is more likely to occur when you clarify what you do, how you do it, with whom you work best, and so on.* Clarity allows you to focus your efforts, your resources, and your energies. It also allows you to craft a message about your coaching business that will attract clients to you (if you are not a secret). Clarity allows you to create a fulfilling practice, as distinct from a *full* practice (we say more about this issue later).

4. *Marketing your coaching business successfully can happen only when you have created the space, time, and energy for this new business paradigm to occur.*

5. *Be a resource.* As you get to know other coaches, professionals, books, and places where your clients can go for specific help or services, you become increasingly valuable. Keep a good database of international professionals, coaches, and schools. You can often find helpful direction or resources for your client with a quick phone call or e-mail. This is impressive because you become a great referral service as well as a coach. And it doesn't take much time or energy if you have the resources and contacts readily available.*

## Marketing Your Practice

In the early stages of developing your coaching business, you can start by getting business cards, creating client folders, and getting ready for your first "customer." We discuss the logistics and pragmatics of setting up your business in the next section. For now, when you are ready to start coaching (and we hope you have had some formal training beyond reading this book), you

---

*We are grateful to the work of Diane Menendez, Ph.D. for many of the ideas in this chapter. Diane is the curriculum developer and lead instructor for the Institute for Life Coach Training. She also assisted in the design of this content with Patrick Williams and Sherry Lowry, the original developers of the Life Coach Training Program of TherapistU, which is now the Institute for Life Coach Training.

need to start trying on the metaphoric coach's uniform. Get accustomed to using the words life coach, personal coach, or business coach. The popularity of coaching makes marketing much easier than it used to be. We cannot stress enough, however, that although you may be able to add coaching to your business and learn much from this book and others, you are not likely to become a masterful life coach without formal coach-specific training, as well as consulting with your own personal coach. (See the information about coach-training programs in the Resources.)

### Developing a Target Niche

The current wisdom in marketing today, especially for a service-oriented business, is to develop one to three target niches. As a therapist or counselor, you may have some special expertise or skills that would lend themselves to a specific niche. For example, if you already do marriage or couples counseling, you could market yourself as a relationship coach. We know many relationship coaches who do couples coaching by phone and attract busy, dual-income couples who want to improve their relationships and often just need the space and time devoted to coaching for transformation to occur.

Another possible niche is family business coaching for a skilled systems-oriented therapist who is knowledgeable about the unique dynamics that arise in family-owned businesses. Associations and specific trainings are available for those who would like to specialize in coaching family businesses. Teen coaching, family coaching, coaching people with ADD, and so on, are other obvious niches for skilled therapists.

We know a former career counselor who now has a full-time coaching business with career coaching as a specialty niche. All she really needed to change was the way she described her business. She still gives traditional assessments and job-search "coaching," but now she can do it internationally through faxes and e-mails. When clients complete their career-specific coaching, they often want to retain her as their life coach; the coaching then takes on a more whole-life perspective.

One way to develop a possible niche is to take a look at who comes into your office now. With what kinds of clients do you work best? Who you enjoy working with the most? On the other hand, many therapists-turned-coaches develop new interests and may not want to do the same type of coaching as the therapy they did. It may also be confusing as to whether you are attracting coachable clients or clients who need therapeutic interventions. Because this can be one of the most challenging areas in your transition, we recommend that you confer with your own coach or mentor.

### Branding versus Niche Development

We have had discussions with many of our trainees in our coach-training business, or with therapists we have mentored to become coaches, about the distinction between *branding* and *niche development.*

Branding is based on the concept of singularity. It creates in the mind of the prospect the perception that no product on the market is quite like your product (Ries & Ries, 1998, p. 7). You are your product. The coaching service you provide is your coaching—your style, your personality, your energy, your insight, and your integrity. Branding as a coach implies that you consider your own unique qualities and the unique qualities of the people you really want to coach, and you then give that combination a brand. For example, Pat is known for his Total Life Coaching™ and Total Life Creation™ approaches to life coaching. Deb is known for Human Dynamics.

One coach we know wants to be known as the "life balance coach" and works with "busy professionals on the go who want to achieve balance in work, family, and fun." That is an example of a branding more than a niche. Next, she might think of a niche market where she could find such busy professionals—for example, lawyers, therapists, entrepreneurs, and so on. Can you see how this could be her entrée into coaching? How do you want to be branded?

---

### ☞ TRY IT! ☜

Ask three friends and three colleagues what they find unique about you and your relationship with them. What do you get from you that is special? You are as unique as a snowflake or a fingerprint. How does that uniqueness impact who you coach and how you coach? How might this uniqueness lead to a *brand*? Write down your thoughts and feedback in your coaching notebook or journal.

---

## *No Matter Where You Go, There You Are*

Marketing can occur all the time because as a therapist (and as a coach), it is you whom people hire, and the "you" that you present in public is part of the marketing. Another way to say this is that you are your message. This does not mean that you are always selling, but it does mean that informal ways of meeting people or having conversations will eventually lead to the ubiquitous question, "What do you do?" How you answer that question or how you even elicit that question is the simplest, most efficient way to market your coaching business. We and many of our colleagues have actually found clients at the local tennis club, at an informal networking meeting, or on an airplane ride. The latter is actually more common than you think! How many times have you conversed with your seatmate on a plane and asked him or her, "What do you do?" If you ask it of your seatmate, he or she will ask it of you. One of the rules of good networking is to be interested in other people. People love to talk about themselves, and if you are genuinely interested in them—what their business is, what their hobbies are, or what dreams they have—they will most likely ask you what you do. Bingo! You might have a potential client.

Another marketing tip is often called the "elevator speech" or "magic moment." It is a quick response for those inevitable times when someone asks, "What do you do?" We like to refer to it as your "laser intro." A laser intro, as its name suggests, is done quickly and gets right to the point. The point is to let people know what you do so that they might ask more questions about how you do what you do. That leads to further conversation, either right then or at a future time, where you have an opportunity to share details about how you work as a life coach and how you might be able to help them. The six key components of an effective laser intro or elevator speech include:

1.  Is it clear? Your response to "What do you do?" must be clear, free of jargon, and easily understood.
2.  Is it concise? A laser intro should be brief and delivered in 15 seconds or less.
3.  Is it compelling or captivating? Your message must have a compelling quality—one that begs further inquiry and piques the listener's interest.

4. Is it conversational? Your message should be delivered in an informal manner. This takes practice. You must be so natural and automatic with your message that it doesn't sound like a rehearsed speech. A message delivered conversationally will encourage further conversation in your audience.

5. Is it delivered with confidence? The more practiced and natural you are, the more confident and passionate you are about what you do, and the more attractive your message is. Remember that *you are your message*.

6. Is the word coach in your message? Somewhere in your message, you must say you are a coach (life coach, business coach, personal coach, relationship coach, parent coach, and so on). It is important for you to provide details about your style of coaching so that the listener can judge whether he or she might be interested in your services.

Having two or three laser intros is important so that you can adapt the basic message to your audience while still describing very quickly what you do. Here are a few tried-and-true laser intros we and other coaches have used successfully.

Q: What do you do?
A: I am a personal life coach. You know how people often have that gap between where they are and where they want to be? I work with them on filling the gap and creating the life they really want.

Q: What is it that you do?
A: Pretty much anything I want on any given day! And I teach others to do it, too! Does that sound like something that might interest you?

Q: What do you do?
A: I am a personal life coach. You know how a plumber comes in and snakes out your pipes to get the water flowing freely? What I do is work with people to unclog the personal and business blocks that keep their lives from flowing freely.

After the laser intro gets attention, hopefully the person might ask something like, "That sounds interesting . . . how do you do that?" Then the door is open to set a meeting over coffee, or better yet, to grant the person a free 30-minute coaching call so he or she can experience it firsthand. Even if you do not gain a client, the person will, at the very least, be familiar with your style and may become a great referral source for you!

In fact, your goal when you network with people or dialogue about your career is to be open to the possibility that the person may be really interested in what you do and may want to know more. It is at this opportunity that we recommend being a living brochure*—don't just talk about what coaching is, demonstrate it. Ask if you can coach the person on something he or she wants to change or some long-term goal. A spot coaching demonstration gives potential clients a taste of coaching, and they may then want the entire menu!

Now that you have a good idea of how you can market your business and build your coaching visibility, it is very helpful to learn some key strategies for your actual marketing plan. You may know what to say and how to say it, but you need people to hear it. Generally speaking, Yellow Pages ads and other traditional advertising methods do not work in this person-centered business. You need to speak with people and network in ways that increase your visibility and expand your geographical market. Remember, in a tele-coaching business, you are not geographically bound. Like many coaches, we have international practices. The whole world is literally your target market!

## Helpful Marketing Ideas

As we said earlier, most of us were not taught business or marketing skills, and we do not like to see ourselves as salespeople. It has been said that opening a relationship is the first step to closing the sale. Marketing your coaching business requires relationship marketing and networking as ways for you to stop being invisible. Have fun, and work with a mentor coach who has made the transition from therapy to coaching successfully. The following tips are included (with permission) as an added bonus to get you stated in launching your coaching business.

---

*This term comes from Robert Alderman, a longtime coach and mentor.

## Marketing Ideas for People Who Hate Selling

The term "marketing" strikes fear and trembling in the hearts of many different professionals! After years of coaching both new and seasoned professionals, I have concluded that marketing simply means "establishing new relationships within the context of doing business." Marketing is the "mother's milk" of successful business development and can produce solid relationships that last long after any kind of business transaction takes place—or even if it doesn't!

What follows is many of the best ideas I have learned from studying with some of the world's best marketers, and from my own personal experience. I strongly suggest you take several of the items that appeal to you from the following list and put them to work for you. Limit yourself to two or three ideas at any one time, and give them a fair trial period to produce the results you desire. Truly effective marketing can be as easy as 1, 2, 3!

### Step #1—Don't Be a Secret

You may already know the old marketing adage, "It's not what you know, but who you know that counts." A more appropriate marketing mantra for the 21st century would be, "It doesn't matter who you know; what truly matters is *who knows about you!*"

In short, don't be a secret! Make it effortless for others to find out about you and about the benefits of doing business with you! Utilize technology to establish ongoing systems for lead generation and referrals!

### Step #2—Be "Interested" Instead of "Interesting"

The truth is, "People don't care how much you know, until they know how much you care!" Make certain your focus is on providing genuine value and service to others and you'll begin to attract new business with ease.

---

The material in this section has been adapted from *Practice Made Perfect: All You Need to Make Money as a Coach* by Dr. James S. Vuocolo (© 2003 by Life Coach Press), and is used with permission.

Focus on being genuinely *interested in others* instead of concentrating on how to be *interesting to others*. Ask lots of questions, and really listen to hear how others are responding around you.

### Step #3—Underpromise, Then Overdeliver—Not the Other Way Around

Promise to give your clients 100%—then deliver 110% all of the time. Do the unexpected. They will love you for it! This step always requires your best efforts—but if you're truly passionate about the business you're in, there's no sacrifice involved.

By utilizing a few of the following ideas, you will attract more prospects and enjoy more profitability than ever before.

Whether you choose a high-tech or low-tech approach, it's important to remember that any effective marketing requires time and persistence. Happy marketing!

## Part I—The Basics: Preparation and Planning

1. **Identify Your Own Vision, Purpose, and Mission:** Envision what you want your business to look like 2–3 years from now (but not any further ahead). Be specific. How much revenue will it produce, and from what sources? Make sure your *vision* reflects your overall *purpose* (reason) for being in business, and that your *mission* (action phase) is in sync with your values and purpose. Otherwise, you will eventually feel "disjointed" and "out of integrity."

2. **Identify Your "Ideal Client/Customer" Type (or Niche):** Make a list of who and what you are looking for in an "ideal client/customer" type. Be specific. Where do they reside? Work? Vacation? Dine? This doesn't necessarily mean you'll refuse to do business with others—merely that, if you had your choice, these are the people with whom you prefer to work. *Hint*: An ideal client or customer is one who "gives" you energy, whereas non-ideal clients are those who inadvertently "sap" or "drain" your energy by working with

them. Be specific, and you'll know where to go in order to network with these people—and life will know precisely who to place in your path.

3. **Develop and Maintain a List:** This is, perhaps, the single most important piece for anyone who is serious about business growth and development. It doesn't matter how great your business ideas or promotional materials are if you don't have a list of prequalified people to contact. Your list needs to include those who have made serious inquiry about your products or services, and not just anyone whom you know. Once people ask for information, ask if they would like to be on your contact lists for future reference, offerings, and information. Let them know there's no cost or obligation, and that they can "unsubscribe" at any time.

4. **Develop a Marketing Plan:** Don't make this rocket science! You can keep it simple and practical yet still be effective. Describe your specific client niche/niches, their locations and numbers, and the precise methods you intend to use to reach them with your message. Include line items for your time and for the money you have budgeted to implement your plan. Set precise goals/intentions that define "success" for you and then track your ongoing results. If you're looking for additional financing, your marketing plan will need to support the stated mission, vision, purpose, and goals of your business. Emphasize that which reflects your particular values and compliments your own behavioral style—then go to work implementing your plan with enthusiasm.

5. **Develop an Authentic Introduction (sometimes called an "elevator speech" or "unique selling proposition, or USP)** that tells others who you are and what you do that makes you unique. Tailor each message to your target audience and offer specific benefits. *Example*: Don't just say "I'm an attorney." Instead, say: "I enjoy helping small business owners easily navigate the ocean of laws and red tape that often surround their candidate selection and termination decisions."

6. **Design a Quality Flyer/Brochure and Business Card:** Maybe no one will choose to do business with you simply because of your business card or brochure, but having high-quality items in this area is essential for in-person sales calls, mailings, speaking engagements, networking groups, workshops, etc.

7. **Place Your Elevator Speech on the Back of Your Business Card:** This way, people know "how to contact you" on the front and "why to contact you" on the back.

8. **Create a "Media Kit":** This is a high-quality folder you can hand out or mail to prospects. Your media kit may contain all or some of the following: your photograph, articles you have written, articles that have been written about you, your brochure, your résumé, a list of questions you are frequently asked and the answers to those questions, your vision, purpose, and mission. It may also include an audio or video tape, and anything else that lets people know who you are and how your services or products may be of benefit to them. Use photographs. People may not always remember names, but they *do* remember faces—which is precisely why photos of missing children are placed on milk cartons and flyers. Place your own photo on business cards, letterhead, and advertising flyers. Also place an electronic image of yourself at your website. Photos help people to feel as if "they know you."

9. **Join a Networking (or Leads) Group:** Networking groups (also called leads groups) hold regular meetings where business people exchange contacts, ideas, and referrals. Ask several business people for their experience regarding such networking groups in your area—or begin your own. (*Note*: This is different from the next idea.)

10. **Join or Start a Mastermind Group:** A mastermind group is three to six friends or colleagues who meet on a regular basis to discuss each others' goals, plans, and dreams. When groups of people come together, ideas are generated in ways that probably would never happen working alone. Utilize your group to think up new ways to

market yourselves and to make referrals to one another. Use this group to hold one another accountable, or hire a group coach to do this for you (in person or on the phone), and you will have created yet another scenario where everyone wins.

11. **Create Strategic Professional Alliances:** Building strategic alliances with other professionals is a fantastic way to grow your business. Identify others whose products or services you believe in. If you're a coach, for example, you may refer new business clients to your own accountant or financial planner so that they can more easily manage their money. The other professional will, in turn, steer new business your way.

12. **Ask for Client Testimonials:** Collecting testimonial letters from clients is a tremendous way to gain insight into your own effectiveness and validation as a professional in addition to obtaining a powerful marketing tool. Testimonials are social proof of your effectiveness. Have several testimonials in your media kit, on your website, and/or in a presentation binder to show when you are meeting with prospective clients.

13. **Create a List of Raving Fans:** Take stock of the people who rave about you, your product, and/or services—these are your raving fans and are your best referral sources. They may be friends, clients, relatives, or associates. Your raving fans will provide you with referrals because they believe in you and what you are doing (and you will send business their way in return). Treat these people well. Never let more than 30 days pass without making contact with each of your fans via phone calls, meeting face to face, or mailing them a personal note or newsletter.

14. **Develop Your Public Speaking Skills:** There are several well-known organizations that can help you develop your public speaking skills. Most have local chapters in major cities that may meet on a weekly or monthly basis, such as Toastmasters (*www.toastmasters.org*), Dale Carnegie (*www.dalecarnegie.com*), etc. Members practice their public speaking skills in front of their peers and have opportunities

to develop a repertoire of topics for use later. Joining such a group also provides further opportunity to meet new people, develop new prospects, or obtain referrals from other members.

15. **Maintain a Great Lifestyle:** A balanced, healthy. and successful lifestyle is always attractive to others. Do whatever you can to become a model of someone who's living a great life. Stop doing things and being with people that drain your energy. Surround yourself, instead, with people and things that give you energy. Identify what areas of life you'll want to improve—for example, relationships, physical fitness, finances, nutrition, boundaries, time off, personal standards, and integrity. Hire a personal and/or business coach to partner with you for successfully meeting your goals.

16. **Identify and Evaluate Your Spending on a Quarterly Basis:** You may be surprised (even shocked) to discover that the money you're wasting in one or more areas of your business could provide the basis for that elusive or nonexistent "marketing budget" you've been meaning to begin. For example, sending reports and files electronically can drastically reduce the printing and/or mailing fees in many business goals. In short, "walk the talk" and others will notice.

17. **Learn How to "Read" Other People:** This step is crucial, in my opinion, if you're going to succeed. By "reading" other people, I am referring to the fact that there are a variety of different behavioral styles in the world. Knowing the basic characteristics of each type will enable you to quickly discern the behavioral style of your prospect and adapt your own behavior, as necessary, in order to more effectively communicate your ideas.

## Part II—Don't Be A Secret

18. **Write Articles:** When your work is published in a magazine, newsletter, or newspaper, you gain both visibility and credibility as an "expert" in your field. Always place your contact information in the pieces you write (although some publications may edit them

out). Place copies of your published articles in your media kit, and mail copies out to your database of clients and prospects.

19. **Give Away Gifts:** People like to receive free specialty gifts with an imprint of your business name, logo, phone number, and website. Many sources provide pens, pencils, mugs, letter openers, bookmarks, rulers, clocks, etc. Send a relevant book or tape to a client or customer. Better yet, have an online or local bookstore do it for you.

20. **Serve on a Business Board or Committee:** Serving on a board or committee related to your business or industry can help you meet the right people to further expand your database, strengthen your professional image, help you acquire new skills, and place you in front of new prospects. (Be sure you know what you're committing to before volunteering!)

21. **Conduct Workshops:** By offering workshop topics related to your business, you can hone your message, meet new prospects, and position yourself as an expert and so, be attractive to new clients. Have an evaluation form for each participant to fill out that includes contact information and a box to check that says, "Please contact me about your coaching products/services."

22. **Hold an Open House:** A special event for your clients, prospective clients, their relatives and friends. Offer snacks and an interactive talk on a topic related to your business or service. Your guests will meet new people, learn valuable information and get to know someone wonderful—you! (*Hint*: Invite the local media to attend.)

23. **Speak at Local Service Clubs:** A great way to gain credibility and visibility is to speak at Rotary clubs, Kiwanis clubs, Lions clubs, and Chamber of Commerce meetings; these groups are always looking for speakers. Deliver a message on a topic you are passionate about and that relates directly to your business. Provide handouts with your contact information (e.g., your phone and fax numbers, e-mail address and website) so that people can reach you later. First impressions are very important. I recommend joining Toastmasters or a Dale Carnegie group in order to develop public speaking skills.

24.  **Make an Audio File:** Find a place with great acoustics or rent some time at a recording studio. Have a friend interview you about your business over the phone and record the conversation. (You can prescript this with a list of questions for your interviewer.) Edit the recording as needed (perhaps add some intro and exit music, etc.). Make copies and you'll have an audiotape, CD, or MP3 file about your products or services that you can give away, mail, or e-mail to new prospects.

25.  **Publish Your Story:** Find a local newspaper or magazine willing to publish a story about you and your business—or write one yourself and ask them to publish it. Often business groups, such as the local Chamber of Commerce, will place a story highlighting the services or products of new members in their publication. Be certain to ask for the reprint rights and post the story on your website, place it in your "media kit, on the back of handouts, etc.

26.  **Host A Radio Show:** Many local radio stations will permit you to develop and maintain your own radio show—especially if you're willing to pay for the time! You can have other businesses sponsor your show by selling them advertising time while your show airs. You can also interview these business owners by having them participate as expert guests, and have people call in, or not, as you prefer. Always ask for your program to be recorded so you can duplicate and mail tapes to existing clients, future prospects, etc.

27.  **Gain Media Attention:** Contact members of the local media and let them know about your areas of expertise and your willingness to serve as a resource if they are producing a story regarding your client niches. Add these persons to your own mailing/fax lists for newsletters and updates about your business. Eventually, you'll probably be contacted for a quote or an interview, which in turn gives you further credibility and visibility. Always ask permission to make copies of such articles for your own media kit.

28.  **Mail Letters:** Send a letter out to your entire mailing list of friends, business contacts, and prospects that explains what you do and how

you do it. You might include a gift certificate for a free sample product or a personal session that they can use or give away to a relative or friend. *Hint*: Instead of simply mailing out hundreds of these letters, mail out only 5–10 per week. Follow up each one with a personal telephone call the following week as you sent out a new batch of 5–10 letters, etc. The personal touch will distinguish you from a typical bulk or "junk" mailer.

29. **Mail Postcards:** Unlike letter and brochures, postcards ALWAYS are read by the recipient . . . and even by letter carriers along the way! Use postcards as a low cost way to effectively promote workshops, seminars, and teleclasses; drive traffic to your website; or introduce new business ideas and services.

30. **Business Card Placement:** Ask a few businesses in your area if they will let you display your business card or brochures/flyers on their counter or bulletin board. This is an effective and low cost way to get your business name out there. (*A special hint for introverts*: Go to the self-help section of your local library or bookstore and give away "bookmarks" by placing your business card in some of the books! It works!)

31. **Use Classified Ads:** This is a low-cost way to advertise on a regular basis. You may want to promote your website or business offerings via a toll-free number with a prerecorded message in which you offer a free coaching session, sample product, or newsletter subscription in exchange for gaining a caller's contact information. This is an effortless way to build your mailing list or database.

32. **Appear on Local Cable TV Shows:** Many cable television stations offer free studio time to local residents. You can simply contact them and submit a proposal. If you create an entertaining and informative show, they may air it throughout your area. If not, they can tell you how to become a guest on someone else's cable show.

33. **Ask up Front for Referrals:** Always ask existing clients, "Who do you know that might benefit from my products/services?" This is a simple yet powerful way to meet new prospects. Let your clients

know that you are seeking to expand your coaching practice. Chances are they would enjoy helping you—especially during the first 30–60 days of your relationship, when they're most excited to be working with you! Always send a thank-you note when a referral is made. You may also send a small gift of appreciation whenever a prospect becomes a client by means of a referral—but first obtain the new client's permission to do so.

34. **Publish a Newsletter:** Give away some valuable information to your readers and your newsletter will get read, be appreciated, and get passed along to others. Having a newsletter establishes you as "an expert" in your field as it grows your database. It also allows you to maintain contact with a growing number of people—an audience with whom to share the benefits of working with you.

35. **Donate Goods and Services to Charities:** Many charitable organizations hold annual fund-raisers or special events (e.g., raffles, auctions). This is a great way to give back to your community and gain visibility at the same time. Most groups will include your contact information and/or promotional materials in exchange for your donation of products or services. Check your local newspapers or ask other business professionals about fund-raisers in your area that may be looking for support through donations of goods or services. *Warning:* Many times people will purchase your services simply to make a charitable donation and have no intention of utilizing your services. Or, they may purchase your service for someone else who does not want to use it. Don't be discouraged— you have opened a door to follow-up communication.

36. **Send Out a Press Release:** A press release is another way to obtain an interview with the print, radio, or television media. Make certain your press release is newsworthy and follows the proper format. (There are books at the library or bookstore on how to structure a press release, as well as information on the Internet.) Telephone targeted recipients and ask if your press release was received. Offer to answer any questions they might have regarding the content.

Maintain contact with editors or reporters via newsletters and mailings. Also let them know that you're a willing resource if they ever need information related to your business or industry.

37. **Publish a Book/Booklet:** Authoring a book is one of the best ways to increase your own visibility and establish credibility as being an expert in your field. You don't have to be another Tom Clancy or write hundreds of pages to become an author. You simply need to write about what you feel passionate about! Begin by writing down vignettes from your business experience. Even self-publishing a small, informative booklet is a simple way to get started. Include your contact information in everything you write, so that readers know how to reach you in several different ways (e.g., telephone, fax, mail, e-mail, website).

38. **Write an E-Book:** This is a very inexpensive way to self-publish and become well known. Offer a free E-book about your area of expertise to your newsletter subscribers, friends, and others. You can easily compile an E-book by putting together a collection of articles you have already written that are of interest to your target audience. Be certain to include a special follow-up offer in your E-book.

39. **Be a Conference Speaker/Presenter:** Conferences can be a tremendous way to share your experience and expertise with others. Some conferences will pay for speakers and/or workshop leaders. Others ask you to volunteer your time. Both ways enable you to meet new prospects and expand your network. This, in turn, may lead to more future business and adds credibility to your work. Always have a short, quality handout that adds value for those who participate in your programs. Include your contact information and watch your numbers grow.

40. **Attend Workshops:** Attending workshops that others conduct enhances your own personal and professional development. It's also another way to market your business while interacting with others whose interests adhere to your own. Indeed, many of them will resemble your own "ideal client" type.

41. **Assist at Someone Else's Workshops/Seminars:** Volunteer to assist at workshops or seminars that you have personally enjoyed. You will learn new material and meet new prospects. Bring plenty of business cards, bookmarks, or other specialty items with your contact information to hand out.

42. **Partner with Bookstores:** Ask local bookstore owners if you can offer a workshop at their location that addresses your areas of expertise. Make sure he or she understands that, in addition to making it a free promotion to the public, you'll be weaving several book suggestions into your presentation that participants can obtain at this very store. Use your presentation to inform attendees how working with you can assist them in putting some ideas from these recommended books into action.

43. **Join a Local Chamber of Commerce or Other Networking Group:** Your local Chamber of Commerce can be a valuable source for lead generation and strategic alliances. So can other groups, such as Business Network International (*www.bni.com*). You may be able to submit articles for their newsletters or offer workshops to other members on your areas of expertise. Group memberships may also signal your community spirit and involvement to new prospects.

44. **Create Bookmarks:** Bookmarks get used over and over again. Plastic or laminated ones work best and can contain a great deal of information about your products or services. Be sure to include your contact information and include your bookmarks with every purchase or mailing.

45. **Volunteer to Serve as a Panelist:** Serving as a panelist at an association or conference meeting gives you both credibility and visibility. The experience can also serve to influence others locally or regionally to utilize you as an "expert" in your field. Contact your industry-specific conference or meetings coordinators and ask if they need panelists for any future programs. Explain what you can offer and let them know you're willing to serve as a future resource.

46. **Develop Handouts to Give Away:** Produce a variety of handouts and giveaways that describe your business, help others to solve specific problems, and provide added value for your existing clients. Give all your clients useful tools, information, and ideas to share with their friends and colleagues—and always include your own contact information on each piece.

47. **Connect with Former Clients:** Many people forget that former customers/clients may be interested in any number of new offerings since they ceased doing business with you. They may also become great sources for new referrals. Contact two or three of your former clients/customers this week. Show a genuine interest in them and their work. Invite them to become an ongoing part of your business research and development program and acknowledge their suggestions (whether you ultimately choose to use their ideas or not). Make following-up with former clients/customers an ongoing part of your business.

48. **Join Industry-Specific National or International Groups/Associations:** Identify the primary worldwide and national resources for your particular business/industry and request information about membership criteria and benefits via their website, surface mail, or telephone. For coaches, this may include the International Coach Federation (*www.coachfederation.org*), the World Association of Business Coaches (*www.wabccoaches.com*), or the International Association of Coaching (*www.certifiedcoach.org*)

49. **List Your Business with Available Referral Services:** An increasing number of professional groups and organizations maintain a referral service through which the public can find the right type or geographic location of their registered members. Some referral services are free, whereas others charge an annual or monthly fee. Before deciding to pay a fee, ask several other professionals who are already listed with a particular referral service if it has helped increase their database, number of new prospects, etc.

50. **Form Marketing Alliances and Joint Business Ventures:** Partnering with colleagues, suppliers, and even competitors to share marketing space with pooled financing isn't a new idea. It's worked for auto dealerships, realtors, nonprofit groups, and others. Such alliances may result in better marketing efforts than any individual business or entrepreneur could readily afford.

51. **Offer "Freebies":** If you have a website, get interviewed on radio or television, or have an article or story published, it's always good to offer something free to your target audience. This is a terrific way to strengthen your relationship with them and be able to legitimately obtain their contact information so you can add them to your mailing list. It also increases the chance of your contact information being included in the article or interview.

52. **Have Breakfast or Lunch with a Prospect:** Do this at least 4 days a week, and you'll guarantee your success. Be sure to be *interested* versus interesting, as described in the Introduction above.

53. **Create a Personal Networking Grid:** This idea is a sure winner. Make a list of 100 different kinds of professionals in your area—for example, one physician (family practice), one dentist, one realtor, one massage therapist, one Internet service provider, etc. Speak with each one personally. Explain that you are putting together a referral database of professionals in the area that you can provide for your own customers/clients, and that you, therefore, want to include the "very best" in each field. Then make a time to interview them for possible inclusion in your referral database. In the process, I guarantee they will want to hear about you and your business as well—another win–win.

54. **Offer Scrip (i.e., Your Own Paper Money):** Many nonprofit organizations offer scrip to their members as a means of raising funds for special projects, youth groups, trips, etc. Members purchase the scrip (i.e., in the form of play money or certificate form) for your products or services at face value from their leaders. The leaders retain whatever percentage agreed upon (typically 5–10%) and

forward the rest to you. Then you, in turn, honor the scrip at face value for goods and/or services when their members come to "cash it in." Everyone wins! (Check with your financial expert, as there may be some tax benefits regarding the percentage you have "donated" to each particular nonprofit organization.)

## Part III—Using "High-Tech" for "High Touch"

55. **Reach Out and Touch Others:** If technology scares you, barter your goods or services with someone who loves it. In the 21st century, it's imperative to use the most cost-effective and efficient means to service clients and reach new prospects locally, nationally, and globally. There simply is no substitute for having great "contact management" software that enables you to track anything about clients/customers you desire. Likewise with fax broadcasting, e-mail, word processing, spread sheets, etc. The resources you allocate in this area will pay for themselves time and again.

56. **Use a Squeeze-Page to Expand Your List:** A squeeze page is a Web page that asks for visitors' contact information in exchange for the information they desire. For example, I ask for your name and e-mail address, and in exchange I permit you to access my website and browse the materials there. You can also use a squeeze page to access a particular area of your site.

57. **Use Auto-Responders for Following Up with Prospects and Clients:** Auto-responders are a low-cost way to develop and send a single message or a series of unlimited messages to your target audience. One auto-responder list may be devoted to your electronic newsletter subscribers whereas another targets those who have purchased a particular product or service.

58. **Develop a CD-ROM Business Card:** The latest innovation is the CD business card that digitally tells the complete visual, audio, or video story of your business on a disc the size of a business card that fits in your prospect's CD-ROM or DVD drive.

59. **Deliver Your Media Kit over the Internet:** It's a good idea to reproduce the items in your media kit electronically with Adobe Acrobat Software (*www.adobe.com*) so that you can easily send this around the world as an e-mail attachment or allow others to download it from your website, regardless of the computer operating system they use.

60. **Voice-Mail Messages:** Effectively utilizing your outgoing voice-mail greeting and message is a simple way to promote your business products or services. Always tell callers what you do and the benefits you offer. If you have a digital voice-mail service, you can program each mailbox with a unique message for each of the major products or services you offer. Always have your recorded message reassure callers that a "live person" will be returning their call in a timely fashion (e.g., within 24 hours).

61. **Develop Prerecorded Toll-Free Voice Messages:** When people are looking for information, they are far more likely to call a toll-free number with a prerecorded message than to call a live person whom, they assume, is there to "sell them something." Setting up a toll-free prerecorded message that explains your business services and invites callers to contact you is a proven way to marketing success.

62. **Develop/Maintain a Website:** A website is simply a marketing tool and will probably not increase your business by itself. Think of your website as being a 21st-century electronic business card or billboard along the Information Superhighway that is capable of introducing your products or services to the world. You must still let people know the name of your site in order to generate "traffic" to it (the number of recorded of "hits" each day/month/year). To maximize the number of visitors to your site, offer free information that adds value and think of new items to add from time to time in order to get repeat visits. Always list your website on stationary, at the end of every e-mail message you send, on outgoing voice-mail messages, on business cards, postcards, flyers, etc. You can even place it on

your vehicle! A website is great for adding credibility to your business. Whenever people call for information, instead of paying to mail flyers and brochures, simply give them your website address, and ask them to get back to you with any additional questions.

63. **Offer an E-mail Newsletter:** An electronic newsletter (via e-mail) is a wonderfully easy and inexpensive way to promote your business products and/or services. It enables you to add value to others, by sharing your knowledge/expertise, and highlighting your role as an expert in your field. Although you may not realize an immediate flood of new business, people will get to know who you are and may eventually use your products or services. Add a "Shameless Plugs" section to your newsletters, faxes, and e-mail signatures to promote new goods or services.

64. **Obtain the Best Equipment You Can Afford:** Your copier, telephone, and faxing services affect the image you present. Computer equipment, business software, desk, chair, lighting, and the like, affect your mood and attitude. These aren't the places to cut back! Nor are they the places to overspend. Check with other professionals in your field. Ask what equipment they use and why. There's no substitute for having the right tools to systematize ongoing and routine tasks. It will save you time, increase productivity, and free you from drudgery.

65. **Answer E-mail ASAP:** An easy way to answer e-mail in a timely fashion is to make a folder called "FAQ" (i.e., "Frequently Asked Questions"). Place your answers to various inquiries there, under appropriate headings, so the next time you're asked about the same topic, all you need do is change a few words rather than rewrite the entire message.

66. **Offer a Free Teleclass:** Sign up for a free bridge line at *www.freeconfernce.com* or *www.freeaudioconferencing.com* and invite people to take a free class regarding a topic of your own choosing. Publicize the teleclass using your newsletter, e-mail lists, postcards, etc. Then offer those who attend a valuable follow-up product or service.

67. **Hold a "Design Call" for R & D:** A design call is simply a conference or bridge call of 6–12 people who are invited and facilitated by a host (you!) to discuss the challenges and opportunities within a particular industry or business. Examples include, but are not limited to, educators, therapists, attorneys, contractors, architects, plumbers, salespersons, or just about any other group. This is a very powerful and cost-effective way of conducting research into developing a new client niche or better serving your existing clients/customers.

68. **E-mail Electronic Greeting Cards for Free:** You can effectively utilize an online greeting card service to customize and send electronic greeting cards for any occasion (including thank-you notes, birthday and anniversary greetings, etc.) to one or all of your clients/customers—for *free*! They receive an e-mail notice that they have a card to "pick up" at a given website address. You can even be notified when they read it! (As in everything, use this amenity in moderation.)

69. **Hire a "Virtual Assistant":** A virtual assistant (VA) can do many, if not most, of the tasks that a secretary or administrative assistant can do but usually for a lot less money because you are contracting for services only. A VA can handle your invoicing, bill paying, travel arrangements, and just about everything else—from most any location! They also know a lot about Web-based marketing for example, designing your website, keeping it well placed on search engines, etc. The digital age once made it possible for me to be in California while my VA did my bookkeeping in Texas, and my CPA completed my state and federal tax returns from an office in Wyoming! (Check it out at *www.AssistU.com*—and tell them I sent you!)

70. **Use Three-Way Calling to Build Credibility:** If you have at least two telephone lines, you can place someone on "hold" while using the second line to call a third party (e.g., a satisfied client/customer, an expert) to help validate the truth of what you are telling a prospect. With one line you can obtain the same result by

contacting your telephone company and ordering a "call conferencing feature." This is an inexpensive way to be able to respond to a question or concern instantly.

71. **"Hold On":** Use the "hold" feature of your business telephone lines to feature any new products or services or provide relevant information. Instead of hearing music, a caller on hold hears your message. Change the content frequently in order to maintain caller interest.

72. **Survey Your Clients/Customers and Prospects:** Use e-mail or fax broadcasting to discover people's attitudes and interests. In return for their participation, offer a free sample product, a booklet, a gift certificate, etc.

73. **Offer a Toll-Free Number for Your Coaching Clients:** This is an inexpensive way to add both value and convenience for out-of-town clients/customers.

74. **Form an Advisory Board:** This can be three to six clients or prospective clients/customers who agree to meet with you by phone on a regular basis. Use them as a sounding board regarding the products/services you offer and your marketing ideas. Treat them well—and they will serve you well in return. Expect and encourage honesty.

75. **Visit Industry-Specific Chat Rooms on the Internet:** There are people who enjoy having the opportunity to chat with someone knowledgeable about your products and services—and who's more qualified than you! *Hint*: Don't just go online looking to impart your wisdom. You'll only come across in a negative way. Actually join a particular chat room for a period of time and as the participants get to know you, they will ask for your input. Much more attractive!

76. **Accept Credit Cards:** This is a proven way of increasing client retention. Accepting credit cards places the clients repeat payment decision on auto-pilot and completely eliminates the "I have not yet received your check" conversation!

77. Accept Credit Cards at Your Website: More people than ever are making purchases on the Internet via credit card. Everything from downloadable software and e-books, to specialty products that need to be shipped can be had in minutes with a few clicks from a keyboard or mouse. Don't be left out!

78. Surf the Internet: Check out "the competition" online. Visit their websites and see what they have to offer. Adapt (don't steal!) great ideas to fit your own situation—and leave the rest. There's no substitute for staying current in cyberspace.

79. "Automate" Your Offerings: Imagine a system that supports multiple websites and offers:

    a. Unlimited auto-responders and broadcast e-mail
    b. Built-in affiliate program software
    c. Digital delivery for e-books and software
    d. Custom contact and survey Web mail forms
    e. Supports 24 different payment gateways
    f. Secure online database
    g. Easy newsletter/ezine management
    h. Tracking for ads, leads, and sales
    i. Built-in "pop-up/under" generator

    Modern "shopping cart technology" can do all of this, and more!

80. **Update the Content of Your Website on a Regular Basis:** You cannot build repeat traffic into your website if you skip this step! People will tell themselves, "Oh, I already know what's there"and will not return *unless* you give them a reason to do so.

## Part IV—Additional Ideas

81. **Attend Online Groups:** Discover people who have gathered together to share common interests or meet common needs by visiting or joining Internet chat groups, communities, forums, blogs,

etc. Check out *www.yahoogroups.com* or *www.googlegroups.com* and sign up for the ones that most interest you or contain members of your target market or niche.

82. **Offer a Free Gift or Prize to Expand Your Database:** Have a place on your website or newsletter that invites others to provide their contact information by filling out a form in exchange for a free tape, booklet, report, etc.

83. **Offer an FAQ Resource:** Compile a list of questions that prospective clients, and others, frequently ask you. Then add your own answers and create a valuable resource that you can mail, hand out or email in order to save you valuable time.

84. **Create a Single-Sheet Handout:** This idea all but replaces the traditional brochure, and is a good deal more flexible and less costly. You can use your own printer to produce exactly the number of pieces you need, and you can personalize them for each target audience. For example, you may have an outline of major speaking points to give out while you address a local service club meeting; or use another to promote a training workshop, teleclass, or other event. You will, of course, have your picture and contact information on each piece.

85. **Quote Cards:** These are either business-card-size or bookmark-size "posters" with some of your favorite quotes on them. They may contain business or motivational topics, poetry, wisdom sayings, or songs. Add your name and contact information on the back. People enjoy these and will hold on to them, thus increasing your visibility. (*Hint*: Plastic or laminated items work best.)

86. **Greeting Cards:** In addition to sending thank-you notes and holiday greetings, prospects and clients enjoy receiving greeting cards with personal or promotional business messages. These can be humorous or not. Always have them preprinted with your contact information.

87. **Create an Idea Log:** Don't let a new idea ruin your focus, but don't lose your good new idea either! Write it down in an Idea Log that

you maintain. If it's still a hot idea in a week or two, then take action (not before).

88. **Make Your Brochure Lasting:** If you want to create a traditional brochure, at least make sure you don't say anything in it that needs to change in 6 months or a year. Brochures are expensive to produce. Make it cost effective and think about your ROI.

89. **When You Find Something that Works, Stick With It:** Do more of what works and less of what doesn't, and you will be well served. It sounds a lot easier than it is in the heat of a new creative idea.

90. **Focus on Repeat Sales to Existing and Former Clients:** These people already know and trust you. Therefore, your marketing efforts are easier—six times easier—and will resonate more with them than with new prospects. (By the way, here are the answers to the question at the beginning of this chapter: *One-time-only buyers* require the most energy; *repeat buyers* require the least; and *long-term big ticket buyers* require a medium effort i.e., more up front, at the beginning, and far less later on; e.g., corporations and larger contracts.)

91. **Leverage Your Intellectual Property:** If you have written an article, you may also have created a report, an audiotape, a flyer, a teleclass idea, a Web page or pages, and more. Instead of always starting from the beginning, realize that putting the same materials in new formats or blending those materials with additional materials can create brand new items.

92. **You Can Reach Anyone on the Planet with One Simple Ingredient—Persistence:** Whether your goal is to reach 10 new prospects or 100—and even if one or more is the CEO of a large corporation—persistence will eventually gain you a hearing. (*Hint*: When you finally do have their attention, be very prepared and have a laser-like presentation.)

93. **Institute a "3-Foot Rule":** Simply put, this personal "rule" states that anybody within 3 feet of you is a potential candidate for striking up a casual conversation or networking effort. Challenge yourself to use this rule in checkout lines at stores, movie theatres, etc.

94. **Phone Past Clients:** I try to do this on a fairly regular basis, at least two to four times per year. It gives me an update about their life and work and communicates caring. It also provides an opportunity for me to share what is new in my own life and work since we last spoke, and has often resulted in finding new resources and even gaining referrals.

95. **Hold a Contest:** This is one of the easiest and creative ways to capture people's contact information, obtain their valuable feedback about an idea you have, and ask permission to place them on your newsletter, or other mailing lists. The "prize" does not have to be huge—but it certainly helps to have something people want. Why not give away a free month of coaching; a portable CD player; a free book or magazine subscription that is industry specific, etc.? It works! And your prize and most anything connected with it is probably tax-deductible as a legitimate business expense.

96. **Join the International Association of Coaches (IAC)** *www.certified-coach.org,* **or the International Coach Federation (ICF)** *www.coachfederation.org:* A professional association of personal and business coaches seeks to preserve the integrity of coaching around the globe. Joining a professional association enables you to gain credibility within the coaching community by means of adhering to a well-defined code of ethics and having a choice of tracks from which to choose for professional credentialing.

97. **Become a Coachville Member:** If you have not already done so, become a registered member at Coachville (*www.coachville.com*). Their coaching forms collection, alone, is well worth taking the time to join. You will add value to your clients and grow yourself at the same time!

98. **Offer a Free or Paid E-Course:** Take your area of passion and expertise and develop a course that can be delivered electronically all at once or in bite-size pieces using auto-responders.

99. **Enable Your Website to Talk:** How about sending an audio postcard via e-mail that features your own voice, or letting visitors to your

website hear a personal welcome greeting. You can now personalize your e-mails and websites with audio. *This is a must-have tool!*

100. **Enable Prospects to *See* You in Action:** Having a video clip of yourself offering a personal greeting or conducting a workshop at your website is no longer in the future . . . the technology is low cost and is here now!

101. **Get a Complete Client Management System Designed for Coaches:** Check out all that the Client Compass Management System (www.clientcompass.com) can do for you. You'll save time and money on a regular basis while adding value to the clients you serve.

## Marketing Checklist

Here is a checklist of the key things to do for great marketing success. Check off each item as you complete your marketing plan—or if it is not relevant to your plan. Have fun with this!

- ☐ Identify Your Vision, Purpose, and Mission
- ☐ Identify Your "Ideal Client/Customer" Type
- ☐ Develop a Marketing Plan
- ☐ Create a unique and authentic Introduction
- ☐ Design a Quality Brochure and Business Card
- ☐ Create a "Media Kit"
- ☐ Join a Networking (or Leads) Group
- ☐ Create Strategic Professional Alliances
- ☐ Create an Advisory Board
- ☐ Ask for Client Testimonials
- ☐ Develop Your Public Speaking Skills
- ☐ Maintain a Great Lifestyle
- ☐ Learn How To "Read" Behavioral Styles
- ☐ Identify and Evaluate Your Spending

☐ Write Articles/Stories/News Releases

☐ Send Letters/Postcards/Coupons/Thank-You Notes

☐ Arrange to Accept Credit Cards

☐ Hire Virtual Assistant/Coach/CPA, etc.

☐ Create and Send Newsletter

☐ Obtain Specialty Give-Away Items

☐ Develop High-Tech/High-Touch "Systems"

☐ Create a Website

☐ Create a Personal Referral Listing

☐ Design the Best Telephone System You Can

☐ Send Gifts/Add Value to Clients/Customers

☐ Learn an "Amazing Formula" That Brings Referrals

☐ "Automate" Your Offerings

☐ Update Your Website Regularly

☐ Create a Single-Sheet Handout

We asked Jim to grant us permission for the previous tips for business development (check out his services at www.soulbusiness.com). Marketing is undoubtedly the most necessary part of succeeding in making a living as a professional coach. If you choose to follow just a few of the tips offered here—and stick to them— you will develop a thriving business.

# Expanding Your Coaching Practice

## ≺ CHAPTER ELEVEN ≻

# Broadening Your Base:
## *Beyond Basic Life Coaching*

*Ain't no man that can avoid being born average,*
*but ain't nobody got to be common.*

—Satchel Paige

The advent of telecoaching and the Internet has erased geographical barriers and enabled coaches to have an international coaching business from a home or portable office. This not only expands your market globally but also creates ways in which you can go beyond the traditional one-on-one coaching model. As a therapist or counselor, you may have found group therapy to be efficient and financially rewarding. The client got more impact for less money and you, as the leader, got a higher hourly fee. The same wisdom holds true for group coaching, and you do not need to limit yourself to in-person groups at your office location. Group coaching can be done by telephone with clients in various states and countries.

There are three unique ways to incorporate group coaching into your practice, whether you do live groups or groups over the telephone*:

1. Group coaching as added value with existing clients
2. Group coaching with a specific market niche (e.g., managers of various branch offices, entrepreneurs in similar businesses, franchise owners from different locales)

---

*For phone groups you will have to rent or own a bridge line. This is a phone number that is reserved exclusively for participants to call and be on the phone at the same time without the hassle of using an operator. See the Resources section for more information.

3. Group coaching using a personal development book as the tool for discussion and exploration

Let's look at practical examples of each of these.

## Group Coaching as Added Value

Many life coaches offer group coaching as an added value for paying clients. For example, you might have a group phone call (also called *teleconferencing*) once a month for all clients to present a coaching goal or a personal or professional challenge. It is a great way to have your clients get to know one another; this can create mastermind thinking that is synergistic. Just like in group therapy, when one person receives coaching on a particular challenge or desire, others most likely will benefit by listening for similar challenges in their own lives. Some coaches schedule group calls as a prelude to "Saturday Clean the Clutter Day"—almost every person de-clutters their office, garage, or closets together. This format can make de-cluttering a fun and interactive way for your clients to create more space in their lives and gain energy. Then schedule the next group call postevent, so that participants can share their joyous comments on their success.

Other group calls with existing clients can focus on any similar theme that comes up for all of them, such as a conversation about marketing or balancing work and life issues. These group calls are easy for you to facilitate, and they will become your best marketing tool as clients shout your praises to their colleagues and friends. We recommend that you conduct these groups free of charge for existing clients for this reason alone.

## Group Coaching with a Specific Market Niche

Many coaches have found it very lucrative to expand their practice to include group coaching with specific niches after they have gained experience and visibility in the coaching field. An example would be to offer group coaching twice a month, for one hour or so, with local business owners. You can easily find them through your Chamber of Commerce. As a coach, you can be very helpful to new entrepreneurs who need to stay focused on the steps that will help them attain increasing success. You are not a business consultant here—just a business coach (or life coach), helping them articulate what they want and what is needed to help them succeed. This is an old-fashioned support group but with people who presumably do not have mental or emotional disorders. It is a coaching group, not a therapy group, even though support is one of the benefits it offers.

When Pat launched his full-time coaching career, he connected with The Center for Business Development at a local community college and proposed the idea of doing group coaching with CEOs of small businesses who could not afford their own board of directors. He formed a group of noncompeting small-business CEOs who met initially for a 1-day, in-person seminar on business coaching; they then participated in a bimonthly 1-hour conference call to create sustainable results over time with major goals for their companies. Exclusive groups such as The Young Presidents, TEC (The Executive Committee), or TAB (The Alternative Board) hire a trained facilitator (coach) for a very high fee and combine in-person meetings with tele-coaching sessions between meetings. Pat designed a group called The Sounding Board™ in which eight CEOs confer during two phone calls each month and half-day in-person meetings four times a year.

Think of the various groups that could benefit from group coaching. What about owners of the same franchise in various parts of the country, such as owners of Mail Boxes Etc. franchises? Couldn't they benefit from a coaching group composed of people trying to build the same business? Of course, they get some mentoring/training from the corporate headquarters, but they often do not have an opportunity to connect with other franchise owners in a less formal, regular way. Keep in mind that group coaching is not about telling people how to run their businesses. They have rules, policies, and regular procedures from their corporate headquarters. The role of coaching is to help them be more focused, more innovative, and more fulfilled in the way they run their life and their business.

## Group Coaching with a Personal Development Book

This is an exciting area of coaching that is becoming more and more popular. Remember, with the use of a teleconference line, you can attract clients from any geographical area and create a rich and stimulating atmosphere for like-minded people who are exploring similar personal goals. We do not believe in reinventing the wheel; you can use an existing book or program if you prefer not to develop unique or new programs or curricula. Requiring all participants to buy the book creates a common background and map for the group. And you are not plagiarizing anything because you require that each participant buy the book you are using as the guide for the group.

Here are some books that lend themselves well to a group-coaching format. Your groups can be time-limited (e.g., for 12 weeks or 6 months), or they can be ongoing with people joining as spaces open and picking up from there.

*Take Time for Your Life and/or Life Makeovers* by Cheryl Richardson. These books, both best-sellers, are very popular because they have practical, doable strategies. Having a coach to walk participants through the assignments is often critical. Reading a good book is not the same as doing what it suggests. Remember that a lot of self-help books become "shelf help," resting on bookshelves having never been used or read completely.

*The Portable Coach: 28 Surefire Strategies for Business and Personal Success* by Thomas Leonard. This book is very easily adapted to a group discussion format and can be delivered as a sequential guide, presented in chapter order. Or it can be used as a just-in-time (in the moment) coaching model for asking the group which of the 28 principles were a success or a challenge in their lives that week. Then the coaching begins!

*Falling Awake: Creating the Life of Your Dreams* by Dave Ellis. This book is jam-packed with dozens of ways to create a more fulfilling life and includes 12 success strategies.

*Life Strategies: Doing What Works, Doing What Matters* by Phil McGraw. Phil is a psychologist and popular television "coach" who calls himself a "life strategist." This book is a commonsense and practical guide that can be a useful resource for group coaching.

*The Artist's Way: A Spiritual Path to Higher Creativity* by Julia Cameron. This book has been used effectively by both therapists and coaches. It encourages the use of a personal journal and includes creative tasks geared toward spontaneity, play, and looking at living as an art form. The book links spiritual development to creativity by showing how to connect with the creative energies of the universe. Since its publication in the mid-1990s, it has spawned a remarkable number of support groups for artists and nonartists dedicated to practicing its prescriptions and exercises. It is a great springboard for a coaching group.

## Specialties in Coaching

The history of coaching discussed in Chapter Two revealed that coaching was originally applied in the corporate environment via executive coaching. The following subsections highlight new niches or specialty applications of coaching, beginning with executive and corporate coaching. You will also read about the very creative approaches of some therapists who have transitioned successfully to coaching in these niches. Our hope is that you find that one of these specialties excites you; then you can contact the coach for more information about his or her approach. Or you may get a creative idea about ways to apply coaching that are not mentioned here. In the future coaches will be found not only in private practice but also in high schools, churches, probation departments, and so on. The range of coaching niches will be limitless.

### Executive and Corporate Coaching

This is where it all began. Coaching for executives and top-level managers has been around since the 1970s, but it dramatically increased in popularity in the latter half of the 20th century and seems poised for tremendous growth as corporations become more "intrapreneurial" in this new millennium. To stay on the leading edge and keep their best top executives, many companies either hire outside coaches for training and coaching or train their managers to function more as coaches than supervisors. Leadership development and mentoring of younger employees also are common uses of coaches today. In fact, there is also "reverse mentoring," wherein younger employees are trained to coach older employees on subjects such as technology, so that older employees do not have to feel behind the times.

Executive and corporate coaching can be very lucrative because it benefits the client company with decreased turnover, more effective management, creation of new products and services, and happier employees—all of which increase the company's profit and growth. This area offers continuously dynamic opportunity for the coach who is comfortable and savvy in the corporate arena. Ideally an executive or corporate coach should have a graduate degree or work experience in business, human resources, or organizational development, coupled with specialized coach training for a corporate environment.

### Retirement Coaching

For many people, retirement means quitting a job for good, utilizing pension and savings, moving to warmer climates or the place they always wanted to live, or spending time playing golf, fishing, and traveling. Isn't that the American dream? Today, due to inheritance, investments, and increased affluence, many professionals are retiring earlier. And as we predicted in the first edition of this book (2002), the cavalcade of baby boomers approaching retirement age began increasing exponentially in 2007. It has been baby boomers who hire personal coaches, for the most part, so it makes sense that retirement coaching will become a niche or specialty area, sooner rather than later. In fact, we prefer to call this niche "protirement coaching" (Hudson, 1999a). Protirement, in our view, sounds similar to what Carl Jung professed that the latter half of life should be: a pursuit of meaning and purpose and a consciousness of the legacy one is leaving to future generations (Jung, 1953). Some call this "moving from aging to saging"—being available to mentor, coach, teach, create, and inspire younger generations.

We believe that protirement coaching can have a powerful impact on the individual and society. Furthermore, it is fun for the coach, because these clients have assumedly already "made it," and the coaching is more about legacy and creativity than it is about career, life challenges, or transitions, as with younger clients. Remember, this time period is the opportunity for people to do exactly what they want to do, whether they need income or not. Protirement is doing your life's work by living a full and fulfilling life.

# Beyond Basic Coaching

## *Coaching International Clients*

Many coaches have clients from different countries. Indeed, that diversity is one of the joys of telephone coaching. There is also a niche in coaching employees of international companies who are sent to foreign countries for extended periods of their lives. That adjustment can sometimes be challenging, and having a coach who understands and can assist with planning a smooth transition can be very helpful.

Coaching internationally may also mean coaching foreigners who have a different cultural heritage; you should train for this aspect by learning about other personality and cultural styles, as well as possibly learning other languages. Coaching internationally also can lead to travel and consulting or training opportunities. Specialized courses are available on international coaching, or you might consider hiring a mentor coach who coaches international companies and clients.

## *Relationship Coaching*

One specialty area that has become popular is relationship coaching. After all, isn't much of marriage and couples work psychoeducational? We believe that many relationships could be helped to be more loving, purposeful, and satisfying if couples understood that having a coach can occasionally be beneficial, even when the relationship is not in trouble. Haven't we always hoped couples would access couples counseling before reaching a crisis or difficult challenge in their relationship?

Relationship coaching has more appeal than couples counseling (especially to men) and does not carry a stigma; it can be viewed as a skill-building, stress-reducing service. Therefore, we believe that more couples will seek it as it becomes more available and publicized. Of course, some couples will need more intense therapy, but many couples (and singles) simply need regularly scheduled visits with a relationship coach in order to be taught and guided on how to hold open dialogues.

Many life coaches will refer their clients to relationship coaches for specialized work. Relationship coaching can be utilized even when either of the partners has another coach for business or personal life goals. We both (as do many coaches we know) refer clients to short-term relationship coaching as part of their overall life plans. Many busy coaches also hire their own relationship coach because they know how easy it is to lose focus on having the most loving and joyful relationship possible. Relationship coaching could become available and utilized as one would other "maintenance programs" in one's life. Why not have an annual relationship checkup and then get tune-ups as needed?

One of our colleagues, David Steele (who can be reached at *www.relation-shipcoachinginstitute.com*), has even built a niche specializing in coaching singles and teaching counselors and coaches how to work with singles. He believes it is valuable and important to coach singles on how to find the right relationship and then how to maintain that relationship in a healthy fashion. Relationship coaching and singles coaching are really coaching, teaching, and guiding all wrapped into one. Consider how many couples now both work amid great stress and less time and you will see a potentially huge niche for coaches to make significant contributions to people's lives. Therapists trained in Imago Theory (Hendrix, 1988), John Gottman's Four Horsemen of the Apocalypse work (1976, 1999; Gottman & Silver, 1994)), or Michele Weiner-Davis's Divorce Busting (1992), and others, can easily transition those techniques and strategies into coaching couples. Relationship coaching helps couples maintain outstanding relationships, not tolerate mediocre ones.

Lisa Kramer, one of the senior faculty at the Institute for Life Coach Training, has created a niche for relationship coaching, teaches an advanced course in it, and has written on the subject of intentional and conscious partnerships (see *www.lovingwithintention.com*). Pat's friend and colleague Edward Shea also is a great resource for coaches and clients. He has been applying a coach-based approach of Imago Theory to his relationship work for 25 years. See his website at *www.healthyrelating.com*.

## Coaching Students

Several of our colleagues coach students in adjusting and applying themselves to college, career planning, or life, in general. Many parents are happy to pay for their children to have a coach and again, there is no stigma as there may be with having a therapist. Other coaches work within a school setting; for example, one coach we know has developed coaching groups in her college counseling center that focus on career planning, relationships, or anything else that students want to explore.

Another colleague coaches students with special needs through her community college office, providing support to individuals with psychological or neurological disabilities. These students benefit greatly from the coaching by gaining self-esteem, creative ideas for their lives, and improved relationships and personal responsibility. This coach helps students learn how to uncover their unique gifts and talents and adapt to their disabilities.

Teen coaching, as a subspecialty of coaching students, is another natural extension of coaching for therapists who have worked with teens in their clinical practices. Teen coaching is for those adolescents who straddle the proverbial fence—stuck between dependent, experimental childhood and independent, responsible adulthood. Both parents and teens are challenged by the transition during this phase of keeping control versus letting go. Many parents embrace coaching; for fathers and teens, it is an especially positive way to become the best they can, as both individuals and family members. Teens often view coaching as an opportunity to initiate their own path, outside of the immediate scrutiny and volition of their parents. Wouldn't we all have benefited from a formal coaching relationship at some point during our formative years?

## Parent/Family Coaching

Another area that seems like a natural transition for therapists-turned-coaches is parent and family coaching. How much of what you do in the areas of parenting classes, child therapy, and family work could be provided under the umbrella of parent and family coaching? Once again, families that perceive a stigma to therapy may find the prospect of coaching services more palatable. We know several colleagues who offer special coaching services such as in-person groups, workshops, and follow-up family coaching, either face-to-face or by telephone. Like relationship coaching, parent and family coaching can be presented as short-term, information-rich coaching that can family members to understand the dynamics of healthy family functioning and give them the opportunity to design, create, and dialogue about how they want family life to be. We see family coaching as an incredible opportunity for coaches and families in the new millennium as they change in our rapidly evolving society.

## Family Business Coaching

Therapists trained as family practitioners in systemic thinking and strategic approaches are very valuable to clients with family-owned businesses. Family businesses present unique challenges because family dynamics are added to the already existing complexities and pressures of entrepreneurial endeavors. Problems can include harmful expectations of family members; family members working in a business by default, not always by choice; personality conflicts over job roles; disagreements over income, and so on. We believe that coaches with experience as family therapists bring incredible knowledge and skills to the prospect of working with clients that have family-owned businesses, which general life coaches cannot always deliver. Also, organizations and associations related to family-owned businesses can give family business coaches opportunities to write, speak, train, and create products that can increase knowledge of this niche in coaching.

## Using Assessments in Coaching

Many therapists have been trained in the use of assessments. These can run the gamut of personality assessments, IQ tests, interest testing, and even projective testing (requiring the interpretation of underlying unconscious complexes and personality disorders).

Many assessments that are useful in coaching carry no diagnostic labeling and are used primarily in expanding clients' views of personality styles or behavioral tendencies that could help or hinder certain aspects of their lives. The most common coaching assessments are the Myers–Briggs Type Indicator, DISC behavioral assessment and values assessment (both based on early theories of Carl Jung), the Firo-B (Fundamental Interpersonal Relations Orientation Behavior), the 16PF (Sixteen Personality Factor Questionnaire), and the 360-degree assessment (used in corporate and small business coaching) for both individuals and corporate teams or management, and the very popular EQI, Emotional Intelligence Inventory. One of our colleagues, Mike Lillibridge, has developed The PeopleMap, a quick assessment with six different personality types that lends itself extremely well to coaching. (See Resources for information on obtaining these assessments).

Handled by a skillful coach, the results of these assessments can be enlightening and transformational. Handled by a novice or someone untrained in human dynamics, they can be disastrous and wounding. We believe that mental health professionals familiar with group dynamics and the art of communicating assessment data can become strong coaches in this area. We also believe that some advanced training in using assessments may be required in order to use these assessment approaches in the coaching process. These assessments all gather information about tendencies or behaviors that may help a client or corporate team understand how some strengths in certain contexts may be weaknesses in other contexts. Just as a right-handed person could learn to use his or her left hand if it were necessary, people can learn where their natural tendencies are best applied and how to adapt or improve different behaviors. The use of assessments in coaching should expand and clarify clients' possibilities for excelling and, when necessary, point out problem areas for learning, training, and coaching.

As you can see, coaching can be applied in special approaches and in many ways. The possibilities are really endless: the examples presented in this chapter are just a few options. Use your imagination, work with your coach, and create a way to coach that rekindles your life's passion.

# CHAPTER TWELVE

# Self-care for Life Coaches

*Live with Intention*
*Walk to the Edge*
*Listen Hard*
*Practice Wellness*
*Play with Abandon*
*LAUGH*
*Choose with no regret*
*Appreciate your friends*
*Do what you love*
*Live as if this is all there is*
—Maryanne Radmacher-Hershey

Despite all the good qualities of the coaching profession, we have encountered some coaches who are experiencing increasing stress and anxiety, a sense of being overwhelmed, and frustration with the new work life they have created for themselves. This concerns us. How can life coaches maintain zest and enthusiasm for their work and avoid the burnout that many of us encountered in our previous lives as therapists and other helping professionals? This chapter examines the concept of coach self-care from the holistic perspective of wellness. Burnout is described and coaches' stories are shared to illustrate what happens when one's life is out of balance. Recommendations from practicing life coaches are offered to guide you as you begin or renew a self-care commitment.

## Burnout

Over the past decade, most of us have encountered therapists and other colleagues whom we would call "burned out." Perhaps even you have experienced the realization that it is no longer fun or fulfilling to do the type of helping work that was once the love of your life. Even worse, maybe this feeling became a constant stress on your health and relationships. We wonder how helpers, who are doing so much to improve the human condition, can be in such sad shape themselves? More specifically, why do some life coaches find themselves falling into the same burnout trap that motivated them to leave therapy and other helping professions? Could it be they thought working with a "healthy" population would somehow immunize them to stress-related afflictions? Did they think that setting their own schedule and coaching from home would free them from the overload and frustration they had encountered in their previous line of work? Whatever the reason, we know that believing coaches are invincible to the stresses and toils of other helping professionals is an error that can be costly to your wellness and your coaching practice.

Life coaching is not a stress-free practice. If you aren't cautious, you can end up burned out. However, coach burnout appears to be limited when we consider all the life coaches we know and have mentored. Between us we have mentored over 100 coaches. Coaching as a career seems to energize rather than lead to burnout. The only way burnout occurs with coaches is if they are working outside their own limits and boundaries—a practice that is counterproductive to good coaching. We are unsure whether this low level of burnout is simply our isolated experience, but we would speculate that it is related to the unique characteristics of the life coaching profession; the level of experience, preparation, and resilience that therapist-trained coaches bring to a life coaching practice; and the newness of the profession. Clearly, this topic deserves more study and investigation. For the purpose of this book, we believe that a brief review of burnout is important and that a proactive approach to the issue of coach self-care would benefit us all.

The following stories, shared with us by life coaches describing how they felt about their coaching practices, illustrate coach burnout.

### Coach #1

I loved my training and was so thrilled to start my coaching practice. I successfully maintained both part-time therapy and coaching practices for 6 months. I was good at balancing everything and my practice thrived. It seemed as if in no time I had more therapy clients and more coaching clients than I could really handle. Then one of my therapy clients attempted suicide, and I really got behind on my other appointments, both therapy and coaching. Soon it seemed as though all I was doing was rescheduling and juggling. A couple of clients left, and I stopped working with my mentor coach because I just couldn't find time. Then my daughter got sick, I got sick, and suddenly one day I awoke and realized this wasn't fun any more. Where did I go wrong?

### Coach #2

Initially I loved my life coaching practice and was so relieved to be out of therapy and managed care restrictions. Plus, I got to work with healthy individuals on my own terms and schedule. Soon I was traveling, doing some workshops for organizations, and having a lot of fun. I would talk to my clients on the phone at airports and on the road in my car. When I picked up some international clients, I found it increasingly difficult to schedule them into my day and travel, as I wanted to, across time zones. I originally liked the flexibility of my work, but I began to notice that I could never get away from my coaching practice. With therapy, I could at least close the door. This isn't as much fun as it was in the beginning.

These examples of existing or impending burnout are reminders to us that even life coaches, with all their great opportunities and knowledge, must be aware of the signs of burnout. We can implement proactive strategies in our personal and professional lives before burnout becomes a problem. Let's review some of the literature on burnout to determine its applicability to our work as life coaches.

## Helping Professional Burnout

Burnout was recognized as a serious cause of impairment among helping professionals in the late 1970s, and it continues to be a matter for concern (Capner & Caltabiano, 1993; Farber, 1990; Figley, 1993; Schaufeli, Maslach, & Marek, 1993). Although there is no standard definition of burnout, Freudenberger, considered by many to be the term's originator, described it as "failing, wearing out or becoming exhausted through excessive demands on energy, strength, or resources" (1974, p. 73). Maslach (1982) stated that burnout is "a syndrome of emotional exhaustion, depersonalization and reduced personal accomplishment that can occur among individuals who 'do people work' of some kind" (p. 1). Life coaches certainly face the chronic emotional challenge of dealing intensively with other human beings, particularly when these individuals struggle to find their way and create the lives of their dreams.

Maslach (1982) further identified common threads in the varying definitions of burnout by generalizing that burnout is a negative internal psychological experience involving feelings, attitudes, motives, and expectations. Burnout can be considered one type of job stress. Although it has some of the same deleterious effects as other stress responses, burnout is unique in that the stress arises from the social interaction between the helper and recipient. At the heart of the burnout syndrome is a pattern of emotional overload and subsequent emotional exhaustion. For example, a life coach might become emotionally overinvolved with client concerns or challenges, overextend herself, and then feel overwhelmed by the client's demands. The coach feels drained and used up, lacking the energy to face another day. Emotional resources are depleted, and there is no source of replenishment in sight. The following quote helps us understand the experience of emotional exhaustion.

### Coach #3

Everyday I was knocking myself out in my coaching practice—for the clients particularly, but also to prove to others (and myself) that I was a good coach. Before the day was even over, I was exhausted and emotionally drained. I just wanted to sit on the couch and cry. I needed a rest but couldn't seem to get away from the endless demands for my time. I felt so alone.

This emotional exhaustion is a common condition associated with the burnout syndrome. Once the emotional exhaustion sets in, helpers often feel they are unable to give anymore of themselves.

This development of a detached, indifferent response and disregard for others' needs and feelings marks a second characteristic of the burnout syndrome: depersonalization. Maslach (1982) reports that when individuals become soured by the press of humanity, they wish, at times, that other people would "get out of [their lives] and just leave [them] alone" (p. 77).

In the life coaching environment, it is not uncommon for coaches to encourage clients to check in anytime and discuss what's going on. Additionally, they support clients with supplemental handouts, reading assignments, or e-mails. If coaches do not set effective boundaries and monitor their commitments carefully, burnout may ensue. For any helping professional who experiences burnout, the almost constant contact with clients becomes too much. Seriously impaired helping professionals may even begin to resent the clients from whom there appears to be no escape.

### Coach #4

I began to get extremely frustrated when clients would call or e-mail me between appointments, even though I'd told them it was okay when we started and I'd be sure to respond quickly. I found myself caring less and developing a negative attitude. I didn't even want to return voice-mail messages from clients to whom, only months before, I'd given huge amounts of time and attention.

Feelings of negativity toward others turn into negativity toward oneself. Caregivers often feel ashamed or guilty about the way they have treated or thought about others; they sense that they are becoming the uncaring, cold type of person no one, especially they, themselves, wants to be around. Here, the third factor of burnout appears: a feeling of reduced personal accomplishment. Helping professionals may begin to develop a sense of inadequacy about their ability to relate to clients, which may result in the belief that they are a "failure." With this decline in self-esteem, depression may follow. Some coaches will seek assistance or be fortunate enough to have caring colleagues who intervene and help them gain perspective and balance. Others may leave coaching and abandon the work that they thought they'd loved so much. Sadly, the problem may well be that they loved their work too much and lost perspective on the critical and holistic balance so necessary for well-being.

## Coach Wellness and Self-Care

Wellness is not a one-shot effort, a here-and-now philosophy. It promises an enhanced life-style, beginning at any point when deliberate conscious choices toward wellness are made. Given the integrated nature of human functions, any positive changes in any one aspect of functioning will lead to enhanced functioning in all areas. (Myers, 1991, p. 185)

Today, bookstores are brimming with self-help books, tapes, guides, and resources to support anyone seeking a wellness perspective. Physical health issues have received more attention partly because physical illness is often the consequence of neglecting health and wellness activities. Health clubs, personal trainers, weight-loss groups, and physical fitness fund-raisers, such as walks and races, are becoming more popular across the nation. Increasingly, popular and professional literature emphasizes the important roles that spirituality, mental health, social adjustment, and other wellness dimensions play in a healthy, balanced lifestyle. Considerations of well-being and self-care are prominent in society at large and require the attention of life coaches. L i f e is full, the pace is fast, and it even seems to be accelerating. Does it have to be this way? For many, the desire to end this craziness is strong. It is no surprise that books on simplicity are so popular these days. It is critical for life coaches to remember that, just like our clients, we have choices about how we live our lives and how we spend our time. We can continue doing things the way we do them and hope it gets better, or we can make necessary changes now.

## Knowing versus Doing

We recognize that most of you who read this book know about burnout. You also probably know how to set boundaries, eat right, exercise, and practice great self-care. Please remember: There is a world of difference between *knowing* what to do and actually *doing* it! This is one reason why people need life coaches.

Bill Phillips describes a phenomenon in his book *Body for Life* (1999) in regard to people who said they wanted to start wellness programs. Many of the clients with whom he worked had all the knowledge they needed to begin a practice of healthy eating and regular exercise. They knew what they needed to do and yet repeatedly did not take action, or they quickly sabotaged their efforts by doing things they knew were not in their best interests. He calls this phenomenon "crossing the abyss." What he believes happens, and we certainly concur, is that people lack the ability to apply the knowledge. The same thing may happen with life coaches who begin to burn out. Without the ability to apply what you know, it doesn't matter how much you know—you'll still be stranded at the edge of an infinite abyss.

So how do you, as a helping professional considering a transition to life coaching (or as a practicing life coach), cross the abyss of knowing about burnout and self-care to actually implementing it in your practice development? Let's take a look at where you are now.

---

### ☞ TRY IT! ☜

Take out your journal and answer the following question. For you to be pleased with your level of self-care, list the five most important, specific accomplishments you want to make—and intend to take on—within the next 4 weeks.

Take a few minutes to think about this, and then list the accomplishments:

1.
2.
3.
4.
5.

---

It is a good sign if you found it easy to identify five specific actions you know you want to take between today and 4 weeks from today for you to be pleased with your level of self-care. This indicates that you are looking forward with future vision.

If you struggled a bit to come up with five specific things you want to accomplish, but you came up with two or three about which you were really confident, you're on track but there is room for improvement.

If you found it extremely difficult to come up with any answers to the question or if it caught you completely off guard, you are not alone. The truth is, many people have a difficult time answering this simple question because it is not something on which most people focus. But if you really want to implement effective self-care strategies quickly in your life, you must move forward. And in order to move forward, you must look forward.

Looking forward is one of the major principles of life coaching. People whose daily actions are governed primarily by future vision constantly grow. They create, shape, and modify their vision of the future. They create action plans and multiple pathways to get them where they need to go. They monitor their progress and adjust the route if they need to change course. It is like sailing a boat across a lake. Keeping in mind where you want to go (your future) and considering the changes in your environment, you take action to adjust your sails. The key pieces here are the *future vision* and the *action*. They will help you cross the abyss.

So, you've identified the five most important, specific accomplishments you want to make within the next 4 weeks for you to be pleased with your level of self-care. If you haven't, do so now.

Here are some self-care accomplishments that both coaches and clients have told us they'd like to make. Perhaps they will help you think of some that would help you accomplish the level of self-care you desire.

Eat better.
Exercise more.
Stop giving away all my time to others.
Stop working too many hours.
Start flossing my teeth.
Stop drinking too much caffeine.

To help you take action, we suggest that you view what you are doing now with regard to your self-care as a habit. We believe that habits can be changed. We constantly modify our own habits, and we support our clients in doing the same.

---

## ☞ TRY IT! ☜

**Get Specific:** Pick three of the accomplishments you wrote down in your journal and commit to implementing them tomorrow. These are actions you believe will make a profound change in your self-care in the next 4 weeks. Write down specific actions you will take toward your accomplishments. Be specific! The more specific you are about what you want to accomplish, the more likely you will be to reach your goal. Here are some examples of actions:

"Get a massage every 2 weeks" is more specific than "Get some bodywork."

"Eat three servings of vegetables daily" is much more specific than "Eat more vegetables."

"Limit my coaching appointments to my established schedule— no exceptions" is much more specific than "Manage my schedule."

**Monitor Your Progress:** Using a form to monitor your progress is very helpful when you are changing habits. Coaches often provide their clients with forms to document habit change. To increase your likelihood of success, place the form in a prominent spot where you'll be sure to see it every day.

**Get Feedback and Support:** Most of us know from experience how easy it is to plan to implement a change but not follow through on it completely. Usually we are successful for a few days; then something happens and we slip back into old habits.

*continued on next page*

---

A life coach is a valuable support person for the client who wants to change a habit. Similarly, we encourage you to pick carefully several appropriate support resources, but remember at the same time that you are the most effective source of your own support. Getting a coach yourself, if you don't already have one, is an excellent strategy. Faithfully using the habit change form and rewarding your own success will contribute to your progress. You can find examples of forms in *Co-Active Coaching* (Whitworth et. al, 1998, pp. 210–211) and *Falling Awake* (Ellis, 2000, pp. 208–209).

**Practice, Practice, Practice:** Most of us who have therapy backgrounds know that practice is an effective tool for implementing behavioral change. Just like learning any new skill, the self-care habits you want to implement may feel uncomfortable or even completely foreign at first. Even if you experience some discomfort, keep your eye toward the future and keep practicing until the habit becomes natural. If you forget or make a mistake, let go of self-criticism and get right back to your daily tracking. Specific strategies you can start using today to help you reach your self-care goals include monitoring your progress with the habit change form, using appropriate feedback and support, and practicing without blame.

## Self-Care Strategies from Practicing Life Coaches

We asked the faculty of and graduates from the Institute of Life Coach Training to share some of their self-care recommendations. The number of responses was overwhelming. We were delighted to read about the effective strategies these people employed in both their personal and coaching lives. We've included some specific responses that we felt could help you get a clearer picture of what we mean by self-care and the variety of ways individuals implement it in their lives. We've also grouped the frequently repeated suggestions together for your benefit.

Here are what some of our life coaches have to say about self-care for your coaching practice.

*Strategies for Balance by Jan Boxer*

One week on/one week off—because I have both a private practice (career and life coaching) and a corporate practice where I manage larger retainer-type contracts, I organize my time by spending 1 week focusing on private clients, then the next on corporate clients. On average I see (or telephone) each coaching client twice per month.

I hold a case-management–type meeting with the coaches who subcontract from me (on the corporate side) once per month. We meet faithfully, even if we don't think there is much of an agenda, because it creates the opportunity to learn from one another. This collegial time fills me up emotionally and intellectually, reduces my stress by systematically providing me with a check-in time, and allows me to feel ready to account to the organizational client, as necessary. Because I am working with other experienced coaches, most of what needs to be communicated about coachee progress or the lack thereof can wait until that meeting. This allows me to exchange sporadic telephone and e-mail contact with the coaches for something richer.

I never conduct more than two appointments back to back (assuming each appointment lasts for 1½–2 hours).

I take brief notes at the end of each session (some notes during as well), capturing the highlights of the discussion and the agreements about homework. This is usually a 5-minute investment of time. I seldom feel panicked because of a lack of recall.

My favorite—taking clients outside! My corporate clients especially love this. We take walks, sit in the park, or share lunch at a café. This helps me to maintain my energy, but it also helps them. They relax more than they do in an office, and I get to the deeper stuff faster. I have been accused of using this as a "technique." Clients often realize that they have shared more intimately in these non-workplace settings than they would have in a business setting.

I make it known that I typically return calls between 5:00 and 6:00 P.M. and can usually be reached in my office at that time. I request that when leaving messages or e-mail that the caller or writer leave several options for meeting times. Once I have established a relationship (meaning, we've met once or twice for an hourly fee), I move to a retainer agreement and a standing appointment (e.g., every other Wednesday at 10:00 A.M.). This simplifies method scheduling and eliminates tons of "telephone tag."

I further protect myself by being clear about contracting, pricing, payment structures, and so on. I use a separate financial agreement and outline the development program in another document.

On vacation I do not check voice-mail or do anything related to work (except read).

When I am overwhelmed with commitments or my workload, I take a "time out" on all meetings that aren't urgent. Sometimes I take a 3-month hiatus—I stop going to association meetings, networking events, book clubs, and some volunteer activities for a period of time. I find I have never missed as much as I imagined I would, and the respite allows me to regain my focus and realign my priorities. I let group leaders know of my intent to return at a later date and thus far have not suffered any repercussions (such as losing a client or impacting the overall contract).

*Love Yourself by Roz Van Meter*

I have a female client from Taiwan who has succeeded brilliantly in a mostly male industry. We were talking about taking care of yourself, and I used the expression "love yourself." She said her family— indeed, her culture—didn't teach children how to do that. "How do you love yourself?" she asked. I hesitated for a moment, gathering my thoughts. How, indeed, do I love myself? I realized that I, too, had had to learn it as an adult. I told her about the following actions that I practice for self-care.

1. When I look in the mirror first thing in the morning, instead of telling myself how bad I look, I say to my reflection, "Bless your heart, you're getting to bed early tonight!"
2. When I leave voice-mail messages for myself, I say, "Hey, babe, don't forget to call Charles first thing tomorrow. 'Bye, Me."

3. I think of myself kindly, as I would a good friend. I try to be accepting and supportive of my efforts and acknowledge my frailties without defensiveness.

4. When I realize I'm in a toxic situation or relationship, I get myself out of there. After many years of always being the advocate for others, I've learned to be the advocate for myself.

After a short silence, my client said—and I could actually hear her beaming—"Thank you, Roz. I just realized I really do take care of myself."

Afterward I thought of all the things I didn't say—comfortable shoes, hugs from loved ones, the deliciousness of saying "no, thanks" when that's the honest answer, lazy days off, shrugging off the small stuff. It's taken me a lifetime to learn, but I do take care of myself. Here are some specific coaching self-care tips:

1. I have become more and more selective about my clients. I honor that little warning signal inside that says, "This person is not a fit for me."

2. Although I do 40-minute coaching calls, I schedule them every hour so I'll have a little decompression time.

3. I crave variety in my work, so along with my coaching business, I also maintain a therapy practice, write articles and books, give seminars, consult with corporations, and mentor emerging coaches.

4. I always build in play time. Every single day. An hour of fun with my husband, reading an intriguing book in bed, watching a favorite old film on TV.

5. I never forget that this is my life—the only one I'm likely to get—and I want to enjoy every minute of it.

### Learn Important Lessons by Andy Viedrah

When I feel as though I'm getting burned out, I focus on making things simple. I feel that stress is just a mindset or perspective.

I have personally gone through burnout two or three times from being a therapist and entrepreneur. The first time was a result of my father's death in 1984 when I had to run his business with his partner until he bought out my mother's interest. I learned some important lessons about life and death.

One of the most important lessons I learned was the power of perspective. This is a little like reframing a bad situation into a good one. I take it down one notch by looking under the frame.

My reality is different from other people because I see life through my eyes only. To me life is like a glass of water; perspective tells you if it is half-empty or half-full. More to the point, it helps you decide if it is really important either way.

### My Self-Care Story by Judy Girard

Self-care is a topic that has become near and dear to me. I had become acquainted with the term "extreme self-care" from Cheryl Richardson's first book, *Take Time for Your Life*. I had been exposed to the concept periodically over the years, but it always seemed to me to be something one did when things in your life weren't going well, like taking a bubble bath to relax when life had become so stressful you couldn't stand it one minute longer. Cheryl introduced me to the idea that this was something you did all the time. I took it seriously and embarked on a new adventure. After spending some time clarifying my values and the things that motivated me, I made some startling decisions in my life and took action.

I realized that not only did I not like what I was doing professionally, it was literally killing me. The constant stress had subjected me to constant physical pain and illness. I was doing some self-care at that time, but it almost felt futile. The futility was that the work I was engaged in was counteracting everything I was doing to care for myself. So, almost immediately, I quit my day job. I had conceptualized that I could do several other things and still survive financially. Part of that decision was a deeply felt belief that amazing things would not happen until I made room in my life for them. As long as I paid attention to things that were not important, I was not paying attention to things that were important. "Where your heart is, there your treasure is, too." There was no room in my life, because it was full of conflict and strife—those were the clients I dealt with each and every day.

I then started to make choices about what I did want in my life. I realized that I had allowed a lot of negative influences to infiltrate my life and that the time I was spending in some areas of my life was not a reflection of what I valued. I signed off of several e-mail distribution lists immediately and cut my e-mail and Internet time drastically. I did sign up for a few new e-mail lists—mostly daily inspirational stuff to help keep me on track.

With the things I had identified as my truest and deepest values as my foundation, I started instituting (or in some cases, continued with) some regular extreme self-care practices. Here are just a few big and little ones:

1. Daily prayer or meditation
2. Modifications in diet—I eliminated caffeine and processed sugar
3. Having lunch at least once a week with a friend or colleague
4. Utilizing my virtual assistant to manage less urgent business matters
5. Simplifying wherever possible—such as celebrating Thanksgiving on a day that's convenient to everybody's schedule
6. Not sweating the small stuff and staying focused

This list may make me seem like a spoiled brat. It sounds self-indulgent—and it is. But as a result, I am happier, more peaceful, more easygoing, and more authentic.

### *Remember You Are Unique by Monte Swan*

Each life coach is unique and should not try to shoehorn him- or herself into a stereotype-model-formula-box. Living someone else's story is the main cause of negative stress in our lives. When we work and live from our own hearts, our lives are genuine, whimsical, and creative. Some things to remember:

1. Overload is caused by imbalance. We were created to rest one day a week.
2. Diet, exercise, rest, and personal relationships need to be balanced delicately.

# Summary of Recommendations for
## *Personal Self-Care*

GET A COACH

If you intend to be a successful life coach, you need a coach. This is the most common recommendation we've received over the years from practicing coaches, especially those who are most successful. Many people beginning a coaching practice have never worked on their own and have no idea how difficult it is to stay focused and on task. A coach who is experienced at running a coaching practice will be a role model. You can learn how to be a better coach through participation in the coaching relationship and also experience what it is like to be a client.

You can locate a coach through a coach-training program such as the Institute for Life Coach Training (see the Resources). If finances are tight at first, other options include sharing coaching with a buddy or triad coaching, wherein A coaches B, B coaches C, and C coaches A in equal amounts of coaching time. When starting, we recommend that you spend time with a seasoned coach or, at least, hire a mentor coach to help you with building your practice.

TAKE TIME FOR DESIGNING YOUR LIFE

Successful life coaches know that having a great life, or at least working toward one, is a characteristic of an effective life coach. This doesn't imply that everything is always perfect for you, but it does mean that you are attentive to creating the life of your dreams. We recommend that you give attention to your whole life and continually create and implement new life plans and visions.

DE-CLUTTER YOUR LIFE

If you intend to make coaching a part of your life, something else will likely need to go. Successful coaches de-clutter their lives, both physically and psychologically. They remove the energy drainers that suck off productive time. The list of energy drainers we discussed earlier is a good place to start looking at areas of your life that might benefit from de-cluttering.

PRACTICE EXTREME SELF-CARE

Again, self-care was high on the list of our coaches' recommendations. Extreme self-care is treating yourself to what you once might have considered a luxury. This is out-of-the-normal, regular, high-quality self-care. Examples might include a month-long vacation every year to someplace you really want to go, a regular massage, weekly manicures, a long bath, or not working until 10:00 a.m. after going to the gym for a workout and sauna. Another recommendation is to develop positive daily rituals that you choose to do. This might be meditation, journal writing, or anything that allows you to connect with your spiritual being.

PRACTICE PHYSICAL WELL-BEING AND MANAGE STRESS

Physical well-being and managing stress go hand in hand; both are forms of self-care, but our coaches set them apart for special emphasis. Eating well and getting exercise will help you manage stress. You should also practice lifetime wellness behaviors. If you aren't currently doing these, "crossing the abyss" from knowing to doing will be a valuable lesson for you as well as providing you with an important experience to share with your clients.

GET SUPPORT

Our coaches suggest that you carefully explain what you do to friends and family so they can understand your job and how it differs from therapy (if that was your previous line of work). This is especially important if you will be working from a home office. In this case, speaking with colleagues who have home offices can be especially valuable in learning and avoiding some of the pitfalls of working at home.

STRENGTHEN YOUR BOUNDARIES

You'll need strong boundaries to maintain a successful coaching practice and avoid burnout. You'll need to make time for your coaching practice and your life. Learn to say no unless the answer is definitely yes. Control your appointments and use your day—don't let your day use you. Go back and clarify your coaching practice and self-care visions. If it isn't what you want and doesn't fit into your future plans . . . don't do it!

### Business Self-Care

Our life coaches had numerous suggestions about taking care of your business. We have listed some here.

MANAGE THE SIZE OF YOUR PRACTICE

When you build your business and determine how often you want to work, stick to it! If you want to add workshops or teach a coaching class, either reduce your number of clients or expand the time and energy you have available for appointments and business activities. Make choices about your coaching practice consciously and in light of your general life goals.

CREATE AN IDEAL CALENDAR

Mark off an ideal time for client appointments and stick to it! Schedule time for self-care and other activities that you want in your life. For example, if you really want to write and morning is a good time for you to think creatively, mark it off.

Some coaches find, as their practice grows, that they work six straight hours with no breaks. One way to avoid this marathon format is to put your breaks on the schedule *before* you schedule your appointments. We highly recommend this practice.

Also, block your clients together on days and times when you want to work, not when they find it most convenient. Having client appointments scattered all over your calendar is frustrating. You will be more energized for your calls and provide more quality time in your schedule for other things you want in your life if you make appointments in blocks of time.

TAKE TIME OFF

Many of our coaches recommend scheduled breaks from your coaching practice. This includes breaks in your coaching day and also days off when you do not work on your coaching business. Self-employed individuals are notorious for not taking time off. Don't fall prey to this trap. Additionally, we highly recommend taking vacations—not working vacations—to get away from it all and do something fun. Plan ahead and put it in your schedule! Many coaches schedule appointments only three weeks a month, which frees up several weeks a year to do office work, marketing, or better yet, take time off.

ALLOW TIME "AROUND" YOUR APPOINTMENTS

Several experienced coaches strongly recommend allowing time for presession focus and postsession reflection between appointments. These buffer zones provide you with a scheduled time to review your client notes from a previous session before the next call or session so you are prepared. Reflection afterward allows thoughtful attention about how the session went and future actions you might take. Jumping from one session immediately into another is a sure recipe for burnout over the long haul.

REFER EXCESS CLIENTS TO OTHER COACHES

Keep a list of coaches you trust who will take referrals. After the initial stages of practice building, our coaches strongly recommend that you develop an active habit of referring clients who don't meet your ideal client profile. Most coach training programs or mentor coaches will help you identify your ideal client. Avoid the trap of taking just anybody, especially when your intuition tells you the client isn't a good fit. Instead, give that person an effective referral to another coach. Likewise, even when you really want to work with a client, refer him or her if you are booked. Unless you will have an opening in the near future, it is fairer for all your clients, as well possible new ones, if you make a referral rather than overloading your practice to the detriment of all . . . including you!

Like everyone else, life coaches need to grow personally and professionally. You've read about some of the activities our coaches practice to care for themselves and some of their recommendations for keeping their practices vibrant. We recommend that your professional growth include membership and participation in the ICF. The ICF is a great source of support for new as well as established coaches, and their annual conference is a wonderful opportunity to take advantage of continuing education opportunities and to network with colleagues.

Before moving on to chapter thirteen to examine the future of life coaching, take time to reflect on your learning about self-care. Complete the Try It! exercise, which will help you determine what you want in your life coaching practice and focus your attention on personal action steps that will help you cross the abyss from knowing to doing.

---

### ☞ TRY IT! ☜

1. What four strategies for having a balanced practice do you want to employ in your life coaching practice? You can use your journal or write them in the space below.

*continued on next page*

---

> 2. What action steps do you intend to take in the next 10 days to help you implement those strategies?
>
> 3. How will you monitor your progress?
>
> 4. Who will you use for support and feedback?

There are many wonderful aspects to the life coaching profession. However, as you've read, the stresses do not disappear just because you leave the traditional therapeutic model. You will need to change how you are with the world and in the world if you truly want to take on an active practice of extreme self-care. We make self-care a daily habit, and our lives are richer and our practices more rewarding because of this important decision.

The following information is generously shared by our friend and colleague, Dr. Michael Arloski, a pioneer in Wellness Education and Wellness Coaching.*

## Personal Wellness Foundation

There are a number of great rationales for continual work on your own Personal Wellness Foundation (PWF):

1. Doing so lends credibility and integrity to your work.
2. Your level of empathy and understanding is increased.
3. You help prevent burnout.
4. You continue to learn as both a provider and a consumer of wellness.

---

*Adapted from Your Personal Wellness Foundation (from *Wellness Coaching for Lasting Lifestyle Change*, by Dr. Michael Arloski, Whole Person Press, 2007). Used with permission.

Your credibility as a wellness coach depends, to a great extent, upon your dedication to your own wellness. This is truly an area where you must "walk your talk." That doesn't mean you have already achieved physical, mental/emotional, and spiritual perfection, or complete self-actualization. It means you *are* dedicated to working on the *process* of improving your lifestyle, your health and well-being, your level of self-actualization. This will be quite evident to your clients and very inspiring to them.

Your ability to appropriately self-disclose about your own wellness journey can be a real asset to the client's coaching experience. The worst coaching comes from someone who comes across as "my story is *the* story" (i.e., the way it is for everyone). However, judicious and strategic use of self-disclosure builds trust and conveys empathy by revealing that you have had (or have) your challenges too. Again, you are the ally, not the expert.

Contrary to what one might imagine, not everyone who becomes a wellness coaching student is in stellar physical condition and optimal health. Not everyone in the wellness field runs marathons, meditates daily, eats a perfect diet, and climbs mountains on the weekends. We all tend, like our clients, to be incredibly . . . human! Our own wellness journeys teach us much that we can then apply to our coaching, but first of all they serve us, ourselves.

Here are some quick guidelines for working on your own PWF:

1. Read and apply "The Ten Tenets of Wellness" (by Michael Arloski, 1994) to your own life. These tenets provide good, basic principles for living your life well.
2. Work with a coach; seems obvious, but it is important to not only buy into this concept and learn from it, but to benefit from it as well.
3. Value every aspect of your life: mind, body, spirit, and environment. Many of us have learned to value only intellectual development. Embrace the side of you that you have been neglecting the most.
4. Make sure your exercise includes all three areas: endurance, strength, and flexibility. Do the things that challenge you and that you tend to avoid.
5. Pay attention to current research and decide what to apply from it to your own life. Remember how the "food pyramid" has been recently turned upside down?

6. Increase connectedness in your life, in every way possible. Lubricate existing connections to friends, family, neighbors, etc. If you are self-employed, this element is especially critical.

7. Make this focus about your personal growth! Get excited about continuing to grow as a person, and much of the motivation to be well in every aspect of your life will follow.

8. Practice "extreme self-care.: Enough with the taking care of everyone else to the exclusion of yourself! Others benefit the most from a healthy and happy you!

9. Write it down. Maintain a personal wellness journal or some kind of method that allows you to keep track of your wellness efforts.

10. Move your body outdoors whenever possible; make the natural world your ally.

11. Discover what "centers" you in your life and do more of it on a regular basis, be it reading, dancing, connecting with friends, gardening, hiking, etc.

12. Remember you are not your work.

Living well and living purposefully are important aspects of being a professional coach. Authenticity and credibility are interconnected in coaching more than in most professions. Coaches need to embrace continual learning and personal development; they also need to value self-care. Additionally, the self-care that you model will be an important means of encouraging your clients to live beyond mediocrity, and to live a life that is purposeful and fully engaged.

# CHAPTER THIRTEEN

# The Future of Coaching

*The future belongs to those who believe in the beauty of their dreams.*
—Eleanor Roosevelt

Is coaching a passing fancy, or is it the true evolution of a new profession? Several indicators point to coaching being a new profession that is establishing itself within the framework of existing helping professions. First, the establishment of a professional organization—the ICF—and associated ethical standards and minimal competencies predict the continuation of this profession. Second, the number of practicing coaches is growing rapidly, clearly in response to the needs and demands of our fast-paced, disconnected society. Third, there is evidence of an increasing number of recognized coach-training organizations and a growing number of college courses and certificate programs on coaching, which further establishes the profession within the mainstream of continuing education for professionals. There are several master's and Ph.D. programs in coaching and will undoubtedly be more in the next few years.

Perhaps coaching would be just a passing fad if not for its widespread appeal to the general population—an appeal that provides a powerful motivation for continued growth and success for individuals and organizations. The growth of the coaching profession, as we indicated earlier, had many of its roots in the corporate world of mentoring and executive coaching. However, in the early 1990s, personal coaching burst upon the scene with the creative vision of Thomas Leonard (founder of Coach University) and some of the other coach-training schools (see the Resources section). The coaching movement has been fueled by the concept and attractiveness of personal coaching. It is a very palatable concept for the self-employed entrepreneur or the corporate refugee who wants to design a life and career that blends with his or her larger life purpose. Coaching continues to grow and evolve in the corporate setting and is a powerful technology for retaining employees, developing leaders, and even transforming the corporate culture of a company. However, we believe that if coaching had only been seen as a corporate phenomenon, it would have rapidly disappeared in the manner of total quality management (TQM), quality circles, T-groups, theory X, theory Y, and other associated "quick fix" strategies. Instead, the quality of well-trained, personally hired coaches, coupled with the internal coaches in corporations, make it increasingly likely that this popular profession will continue to grow in scope and recognition.

Another powerful attraction of life coaching is that having a personal life coach provides a partner who really cares about helping you develop and implement your ideal life. Life coaching also gives a sense of connection, of belonging, of significance in a world that can sometimes seem isolating, overwhelming, or both. Coaches also keep us focused, challenged, and motivated for living our lives (personally and professionally) on purpose. We both have our own coaches for these very reasons.

It is our hope that life coaching, in all its various forms, will begin to permeate society at all levels. We want to see coaches in schools, probation departments, churches, nonprofit corporations, and other community agencies. In reality, this dissemination has already begun to happen. Coaching involves a combination of communication and empowerment that should become ingrained in our entire cultural fabric so that relationships at all levels can implement the coaching paradigm as a new and effective way to bring out the best in people and create solutions to complex problems.

We do believe psychotherapy has played an important role in the lives of many clients and that psychotherapy will still be needed in our society, especially for those who are seriously mentally ill. However, it has also pathologized a significant number of individuals with sometimes meaningless and unnecessary labels. We believe coaching will become the prevailing way to get help or to learn how to bring out strengths and overcome obstacles and challenges while pursuing possibilities. This is what the human potential movement of the 1970s intended. Psychological research and theory of the last several decades have contributed much to our understanding of how people change, how they adjust to life's struggles, and how they develop into self-actualized human beings. Much of this early research and application came from the humanistic and transpersonal branches of psychology. Then cognitive–behavioral psychology offered much in terms of ways to facilitate positive behavior change. Most recently the acceptance and widespread appeal of positive psychology, as created by Dr. Martin Seligman and his followers, has produced new theories of happiness and strength-based approaches to living. That knowledge now lends itself to this expanding field of life coaching, without the stigma and labeling that comes with psychological counseling or therapy. Being able to receive coaching and have a personal coach, whether privately hired or provided by your company or community agency, is a service we hope becomes ubiquitous and transformational to individuals and our culture as a whole.

Another important factor in any new profession in order to be accepted widely is publicity and public awareness. Over the last several years the media have said overwhelmingly positive things about coaching. Many articles have come out about coaching, its impact on and value to clients, and the level of professionalism in the field. In fact, after Pat was interviewed for a magazine article on two different occasions, the reporters asked to set up coaching appointments for themselves. Even though anybody can call him- or herself a coach, the quality of people with this title is very high. Many have come from other professions such as law, ministry, or psychology; others are corporate refugees, human resource professionals, or experienced consultants.

Although many coach-training programs exist and certification is available through the ICF and other programs, certification is not necessary. After all, consultants have never been certified or licensed; they only get continued work through their reputations and previous work histories. However, professional training and strong ethics are important, and there is an ever-growing number of ICF credentialed coaches worldwide as well as coaches who have received quality training from recognized organizations.

We can assume that, as the profession grows, coaching will attract its share of charlatans or unscrupulous business people. But coaches who lack ethics and experience will not last long. The marketplace for coaches is expanding to the point where anyone who is currently a consultant, trainer, minister, manager, or helping professional is either now learning specific coaching skills or expanding the scope of what they offer to include coaching. Coaching has become an umbrella under which many forms of personal services fit.

## Emerging Trends in Coaching

Looking into our crystal ball, we do see some emerging trends that may be on the cutting edge of coaching or may become innovative ways for the public to access the benefits of coaching.

1. *Coach on call.* Sometimes called "spot coaching" or "just-in-time coaching," this is brief coaching available to clients at the moment they need it. A client might have a coach or coaching service on retainer by paying a monthly fee but can call, whenever needed for support, direction, or motivation. Pat is part of a group of coaches, called The Coaching Collective, that provides people with brief conversations by appointment or during set office hours from any one of 12 coaches; clients pay a flat fee of $95 per month to belong to the group. Clients may also participate in classes, book discussions, or a group coaching experience, called Collective Wisdom, wherein four or five coaches, led by a "conductor," offer coaching to one client at a time for 10–15 minutes. As reported by the clients, these brief coaching experiences often lead to breakthroughs. This process is innovative, powerful, and fun.

2. *Videoconference coaching.* Some coaches now coach via e-mail but usually as an added service, not as the primary vehicle for coaching. With the increasing availability of video communication by personal computer, however, this means will increase as a way to connect with clients. There is even technology available that provides virtual classrooms and chat rooms, allowing the instructor or coach the ability to separate participants with different assignments or conversations. Although this technology is still expensive, it will become more mainstream in the years to come. The ease of real-time visual communication via upcoming technologies is going to make global coaching an increasingly available opportunity.

3. *Agency coaches.* We both really see the strong probability of agencies, churches, schools, probation departments, and so on adding staff positions for coaches. What happens in business usually is mirrored in nonprofit agencies and public service agencies.

## What the Future Holds

We are on the verge of a fundamental shift in how and why people seek helpers. People today need connection with a mentor, coach, or guide more than ever before, due to the rapid pace of change, the difficulty of sustaining relationships, and the desire to fulfill one's life purpose.

We believe that the profession of coaching soon will be bigger than psychotherapy. The general public will know the distinction between therapy and coaching and will be clear on when to seek a therapist and when to seek a coach. Coaching will permeate society and be available to everyone—not just executives or high-powered professionals. We expect to see a variety of specialized coaches such as relationship coaches, parenting and family coaches, wellness and health coaches, spiritual development coaches, and others.

The entire profession, as we see it, will foster the idea of life coaching as the umbrella under which all coaching rests. Whether a client seeks specific coaching for business or job challenges, coaching for a life transition (e.g., a career change, relationship loss, health issues), or for pure life-design coaching, it is all life coaching. A coach can also serve as a referral source for specialty coaching, as needed or requested by their client.

Coaching is a profession that is experiencing dynamic growth and change. It will no doubt continue to interact developmentally with social, economic, and political processes; draw on the knowledge base of diverse disciplines; enhance its intellectual and professional maturity; and proceed to establish itself internationally and in mainstream America. If these actions represent the future of coaching, the profession will change in ways that support viability and growth. Life coaching exists because it is helpful, and it will prosper because it can be transformational.

# Common Questions from Aspiring Life Coaches

Q: *Can I transition a therapy client into a coaching client? How?*

A: Current or former clients who see you as a therapist may become qualified coaching clients if they do not have a psychological diagnosis that needs treatment and if they understand that coaching with you is not therapy. We recommend that you have some ritual ending to the therapy relationship and then start anew with a coaching intake packet and meet in a different location or over the telephone. The coaching relationship and coaching services must be seen as separate and unique from psychotherapy. A rule by which we both live and urge therapists to follow is that if a former therapy client decides to hire you as a coach, you should be clear that you can never again be his or her therapist. It is crucial to keep the professions separate, and you cannot be both someone's therapist and coach. You can use coaching skills with a therapy client, but that is not the same as having a professional coaching relationship with him or her.

Q: *What if I start out coaching someone and it becomes clear that he or she also needs therapy?*

A: This is actually a good service of coaching. Many clients can have a coach and engage a therapist concurrently. We suggest you keep very clear boundaries from what is covered in therapy and what happens in coaching. For example, we have coached clients whom we referred to couples therapy, grief work, divorce counseling, and so on, and also have continued to be their life coach. What is important here is that you do not try to be both a therapist and coach. It is unethical as well as confusing to shift between professional roles. Have a coaching conversation about what you are experiencing and discuss your thoughts and reasons with the client and see if he or she agrees.

If, as a coach, you feel it is appropriate to refer your coaching client to a therapist, you might have a conversation with him or her about recommended therapists or at least types of therapy that could be most beneficial. Coach your client on questions to ask, what to look for, and whatever else can help your client find the most appropriate psychotherapist. You can continue to coach him or her if the psychological help is kept separate. If he or she needs therapy before being coachable (i.e., able to make strides toward a desired future), then the coaching can be put on hold.

Q: *Let's say someone comes in for a therapy consultation and I think she could benefit from life coaching instead. How do I handle that?*

A: That is one way a therapist might get some initial coaching clients. Many people come to therapy seeking help with life transitions or a lack of direction in their lives. When life coaching is explained to them and they see that the coach is their partner in designing the life they want to live, they often get excited about the coaching relationship. Again, however, you must be very clear that if they hire you as their life coach, you are not providing psychotherapy or acting as a therapist.

Q: *What are the issues of liability in coaching? Should I carry liability insurance?*

A: Liability in coaching has proven to be extremely minimal, especially if you are clear about not giving advice or professional recommendations. As a coach you are working with clients mutually to decide the steps they want to take, objectives to which they want to commit, and changes they want to make in their lives. Coaching clients are assumed to be capable of making clear personal choices in their life; they should not be emotionally fragile persons.

Liability insurance is available for coaching professionals through the ICF (*www.coachfederation.org*) and through private business insurers. In some cases, therapists and counselors have included coaching in their current professional liability insurance. You must check with your insurer for information on this topic.

Q: *How do I know if I am doing a good job as a coach?*

A: We have two answers: Ask your client, and work with your own coach on this area. It is very powerful to ask your client periodically, "Is the coaching valuable to you?" or "I really want our coaching to be extremely valuable and effective for you. Is there any way I could coach you better?"

Q: *What are the essential details to cover in the first interview or coaching session?*

A: This is covered in detail in a coach-training program, but, in a nutshell, we recommend that you have already sent the client your Welcome Packet, which includes forms for listing desired goals, current energy drainers, things that are frustrating or creating obstacles to the life he or she wants, and so on. Then in the first session, you review these forms and discuss some immediate action steps that will lead to fulfilling any short-term goals that fit with the client's long-term vision and life purpose.

Q: *What do I do if I have a resistant client?*

A: Resistance is a term with which we are very familiar with as therapists. Get it out of your vocabulary in coaching. If you have clients who seem unable to take the desired action steps or keep coming to sessions with no successful follow-through, the next coaching conversation should be about your observations. In other words, as their coach, you are not looking for underlying reasons or neuroses for their "resistance" but instead coaching them toward possibilities and action. If they seem stuck, ask them how the coaching can be changed to help them get what they want. If that does not work, suggest that coaching does not seem to be right for them at that point and to reconsider it when they are ready to make big changes in their life. We call telling the truth and being direct, but not becoming acrimonious or judgmental, a courageous conversation that uses a compassionate edge.

Q: *What do I do if I sense tension in my coaching relationship or if I start to dislike my client?*

A: It is part of the honesty and authenticity of the coach to have a conversation about this matter. As the coach, you model effective communication by not stepping over or around conflict or tension in the relationship. You can actually use this honest conversation as a form of powerful coaching. Frame it as your perception only and ask the client how he or she sees or experiences it. Then collaborate with the client to make the necessary changes.

Q: *Do you have to like your clients to be an effective coach for them?*

A: We really believe that you do. As therapists, this was not necessary, but in coaching, at least for us, we want to work with people we like or at least don't have any negative feelings toward. You will like some clients better than others, but we do believe it is part of the coaching relationship to coach people you really want to work with and whom you really enjoy coaching.

Q: *How does termination with a coaching client compare with termination with a therapy client?*

A: The word *termination* sounds so clinical. In coaching, you do want to formalize the point when the coaching relationship is complete or ending temporarily. But you do not have to be as clinical or detailed as you would be in therapy. You should mutually decide (prompted by the client) that you are ending or stopping the formal coaching relationship, but make it clear that the door is always open. You can trust that your client will give clues as to when coaching is no longer needed or desired. You have the task of frequently checking on the client's perceived value of the coaching, but it is the client who usually determines whether it is time to stop. We do believe that you should consider a final review session that summarizes the coaching progress and then end the session by focusing on the next steps for the client. Let the client know that he or she can always work with you again, or you can refer him or her to another coach.

Q: *Do coaches use some of the techniques from solution-focused therapy, such as scaling questions, the miracle question, or pattern interruption?*

A: Absolutely! Anything you have used as a therapist that can forward a client into action is equally powerful in coaching. Use whatever works from solution-focused techniques, Ericksonian strategies, NLP, cognitive therapy techniques, reality therapy, choice theory, and so on. Many techniques, such as the empty chair technique from gestalt therapy, or cognitive–behavioral techniques, can be adapted to coaching. Remember, you are not treating an illness. You are coaching toward a desired future.

Q: *Do you find that your therapist license is helpful or distracting for clients?*

A: We always recommend that you keep your therapy practice and your coaching business separate. It is great that you have a graduate degree, and that does add to credibility. But coaching clients do not need to know that you are a licensed therapist. If they do, be clear that you are their coach and not their therapist. This separation is also important in order to maintain ethical standards and decrease liability.

Q: *If you offer primarily telephone coaching, how do you make up for the lack of visual cues?*

A. This is one of the real surprises of telephone coaching. We and other coaches have noticed that since we are working with functionally healthy individuals, we do not need to be as tuned into visual clues. In fact, the telephone relationship has fewer distractions and can be more focused than a face-to-face session. You seem to be able to create the necessary intimacy and sacred space in the telephone relationship and use the time efficiently and powerfully. We ask our clients to send us pictures of them, and they can see pictures of us on our websites. These visual aids add to the personal quality in the coaching relationship and provide a visual framework.

Q: *How "self-actualized" do you have to be as a life coach to be successful?*

A: Obviously, you are in the position of being a model for your clients. But that does not mean you have to be a guru or realized master to be a coach! You do, however, need to be aware of the areas in your life that are evolving, and you cannot be an effective coach if your life is in more disarray than your clients' lives. The keys are *awareness* and *action*. If you are working on goals similar to your clients' (e.g., more effective time management, better organization, improved life habits), you can model the path while you are also on it.

Q: *Do you have to live in a major metropolitan area to be a successful personal coach?*

A: In many ways it is easier to make important business connections in a large city, but we know several coaches in very remote rural settings who have full practices. Using your computer and telephone, you can develop a virtual community of contacts around the globe. Marketing a coaching business in a rural locale takes some creative planning and nontraditional ways to get the word out, but in today's high-tech world, it is easier than you might think.

Q: *Can personal coaching be done online via e-mail communication?*

A: Yes. However, neither of us promotes that as the best form of coaching. We feel that telecoaching still has a strong personal connection, and we find that cybercoaching via e-mail exclusively misses that personal touch. However, there are coaches who do online coaching and use chat lines and other real-time formats. E-mail coaching is a great adjunct to regular telephone calls and a valuable added service to a coaching relationship.

Q: *What about the professional ethics and standards of confidentiality to which we are accustomed as therapists?*

A: That is one reason we believe that therapists make such great coaches: They come from a profession that highly values ethics and professional standards. The ICF has created guidelines on the ethics of coaching (see p. 209) and, as a coach, you should always be as ethical as you were as a therapist. Although you always respect the confidentiality of your clients, you will find that clients have less need for confidentiality. Indeed, they are often happy to tell people you are their coach. You can also have friendlier relationships with coaching clients than with therapy clients.

# Resources

## The ICF CODE OF ETHICS

### Part One: The ICF Philosophy of Coaching

The International Coach Federation adheres to a form of coaching that honors the client as the expert in his/her life and work and believes that every client is creative, resourceful, and whole. Standing on this foundation, the coach's responsibility is to:

- Discover, clarify, and align with what the client wants to achieve
- Encourage client self-discovery
- Elicit client-generated solutions and strategies
- Hold the client responsible and accountable

### Part Two: The ICF Definition of Coaching

Professional Coaching is an ongoing professional relationship that helps people produce extraordinary results in their lives, careers, businesses or organizations. Through the process of coaching, clients deepen their learning, improve their performance, and enhance their quality of life.

In each meeting, the client chooses the focus of conversation, while the coach listens and contributes observations and questions. This interaction creates clarity and moves the client into action. Coaching accelerates the client's progress by providing greater focus and awareness of choice. Coaching concentrates on where clients are now and what they are willing to do to get where they want to be in the future. ICF member coaches and ICF credentialed coaches recognize that results are a matter of the client's intentions, choices and actions, supported by the coach's efforts and application of the coaching process.

## *Part Three: The ICF Standards of Ethical Conduct*
### *Professional Conduct At Large*

As a coach:

1) I will conduct myself in a manner that reflects positively upon the coaching profession and I will refrain from engaging in conduct or making statements that may negatively impact the public's understanding or acceptance of coaching as a profession.

2) I will not knowingly make any public statements that are untrue or misleading, or make false claims in any written documents relating to the coaching profession.

3) I will respect different approaches to coaching. I will honor the efforts and contributions of others and not misrepresent them as my own.

4) I will be aware of any issues that may potentially lead to the misuse of my influence by recognizing the nature of coaching and the way in which it may affect the lives of others.

5) I will at all times strive to recognize personal issues that may impair, conflict or interfere with my coaching performance or my professional relationships. Whenever the facts and circumstances necessitate, I will promptly seek professional assistance and determine the action to be taken, including whether it is appropriate to suspend or terminate my coaching relationship(s).

6) As a trainer or supervisor of current and potential coaches, I will conduct myself in accordance with the ICF Code of Ethics in all training and supervisory situations.

7) I will conduct and report research with competence, honesty and within recognized scientific standards. My research will be carried out with the necessary approval or consent from those involved, and with an approach that will reasonably protect participants from any potential harm. All research efforts will be performed in a manner that complies with the laws of the country in which the research is conducted.

8) I will accurately create, maintain, store and dispose of any records of work done in relation to the practice of coaching in a way that promotes confidentiality and complies with any applicable laws.

9) I will use ICF member contact information (email addresses, telephone numbers, etc.) only in the manner and to the extent authorized by the ICF.

## *Professional Conduct With Clients*

10) I will be responsible for setting clear, appropriate, and culturally sensitive boundaries that govern any physical contact that I may have with my clients.

11) I will not become sexually involved with any of my clients.

12) I will construct clear agreements with my clients, and will honor all agreements made in the context of professional coaching relationships.

13) I will ensure that, prior to or at the initial session, my coaching client understands the nature of coaching, the bounds of confidentiality, financial arrangements and other terms of the coaching agreement.

14) I will accurately identify my qualifications, expertise and experience as a coach.

15) I will not intentionally mislead or make false claims about what my client will receive from the coaching process or from me as their coach.

16) I will not give my clients or prospective clients information or advice I know or believe to be misleading.

17) I will not knowingly exploit any aspect of the coach-client relationship for my personal, professional or monetary advantage or benefit.

18) I will respect the client's right to terminate coaching at any point during the process. I will be alert to indications that the client is no longer benefiting from our coaching relationship.

19) If I believe the client would be better served by another coach, or by another resource, I will encourage the client to make a change.

20) I will suggest that my clients seek the services of other professionals when deemed appropriate or necessary.

21) I will take all reasonable steps to notify the appropriate authorities in the event a client discloses an intention to endanger self or others.

## *Confidentiality/Privacy*

22) I will respect the confidentiality of my client's information, except as otherwise authorized by my client, or as required by law.

23) I will obtain agreement from my clients before releasing their names as clients or references, or any other client identifying information.

24) I will obtain agreement from the person being coached before releasing information to another person compensating me.

### *Conflicts of Interest*

25) I will seek to avoid conflicts between my interests and the interests of my clients.

26) Whenever any actual conflict of interest or the potential for a conflict of interest arises, I will openly disclose it and fully discuss with my client how to deal with it in whatever way best serves my client.

27) I will disclose to my client all anticipated compensation from third parties that I may receive for referrals of that client.

28) I will only barter for services, goods or other non-monetary remuneration when it will not impair the coaching relationship.

## *Part Four: The ICF Pledge of Ethics*

As a professional coach, I acknowledge and agree to honor my ethical obligations to my coaching clients and colleagues and to the public at large. I pledge to comply with the ICF Code of Ethics, to treat people with dignity as independent and equal human beings, and to model these standards with those whom I coach. If I breach this Pledge of Ethics or any part of the ICF Code of Ethics, I agree that the ICF in its sole discretion may hold me accountable for so doing. I further agree that my accountability to the ICF for any breach may include loss of my ICF membership and/or my ICF credentials.

# ⋖ The Welcome Packet ⋗

The following pages contain examples of typical forms in a Welcome Packet. You may adapt any of these to suit your needs.

---

Your name and contact information go here

---

## CLIENT POLICIES AND PROCEDURES

### Welcome!

Welcome to coaching as my client. I look forward to working together. There are a few guidelines that I expect clients to maintain in order for our relationship to work. If you have any questions, please call me.

**Fee** — Clients pay me on time unless prior arrangements have been made. Payment may be made by check or credit card.

**Procedure** — My clients call on time. Come to the call with updates, progress, and current challenges. Let me know what you want to work on, and be ready to be coached. Make copies of the enclosed client prep form and fax or e-mail a completed form before each call. The agenda is client generated and coach supported.

**Calls** — Our agreement includes a set amount of calls. If you or I are on vacation, then we spend more time before you/I leave and after you/I return.

**Changes** — My clients give me 24 hours notice if they have to cancel or reschedule a call. If you have an emergency, we will work around it. Otherwise, a missed call is not made up.

**Extra Time** — You may call between sessions if you need "spot coaching," have a problem, or can't wait to share a win with me. (You can also fax or e-mail me.) I enjoy delivering this extra level of service. I do not bill for additional time of this type, but I ask that you please keep the extra calls to 5 or 10 minutes. When you leave a message, let me know if you want a call back or if you are just sharing.

**Problems** — I want you to be satisfied with our relationship. If I ever say or do something that upsets you or doesn't feel right, please bring it up. I promise to do what is necessary to satisfy your coaching needs.

**A Must** — It is necessary for the client to implement the coaching in order to experience success. You have hired a coach to help you do things differently than you have ever done them before. If you choose to not use the coaching and keep doing what you have always done, you will get the results you have always gotten.

## LIFE COACHING AGREEMENT

To my client: Please review, adjust, sign where indicated, and return to me at the above address.

Name _____

Initial term _____ Months, from _____ through _____

Fee $ _____ Per month OR $ _____ For the project

First session date _____ Session time _____

Number of sessions per month _____

Duration _____ (length of scheduled session)

Referred by _____

**Ground rules:**   1. Client calls the coach at the scheduled time.
2. Client pays coaching fees in advance.
3. Client pays for long-distance charges, if any.

1. As a client, I understand and agree that I am fully responsible for my well-being during my coaching calls, including my choices and decisions. I am aware that I can choose to discontinue coaching at any time. I recognize that coaching is not psychotherapy and that professional referrals will be given if needed.

2. I understand that "life coaching" is a relationship I have with my coach that is designed to facilitate the creation/development of personal, professional, and/or business goals and to develop and carry out a strategy/plan for achieving those goals.

3. I understand that life coaching is a comprehensive process that may involve all areas of my life, including work, finances, health, relationships, education, and recreation. I acknowledge that deciding how to handle these issues and implement my choices is exclusively my responsibility.

4. I understand that life coaching does not treat mental disorders as defined by the American Psychiatric Association. I understand that life coaching is not a substitute for counseling, psychotherapy, psychoanalysis, mental health care, or substance abuse treatment, and I will not use it in place of any form of therapy.

5. I promise that if I am currently in therapy or otherwise under the care of a mental health professional, that I have consulted with this person regarding the advisability of working with a life coach and that this person is aware of my decision to proceed with the life coaching relationship.
6. I understand that information will be held as confidential unless I state otherwise, in writing, except as required by law.
7. I understand that certain topics may be anonymously shared with other life-coaching professionals for training or consultation purposes.
8. I understand that life coaching is not to be used in lieu of professional advice. I will seek professional guidance for legal, medical, financial, business, spiritual, or other matters. I understand that all decisions in these areas are exclusively mine, and I acknowledge that my decisions and my actions regarding them are my responsibility.

I have read and agreed to the above.

Client signature _____

Date _____

# The Welcome Packet

## *CLIENT DATA FORM*

Date: _____

Name: _____

Occupation: _____

Business name: _____

Home address: _____ ☐ Preferred address

_____

_____

Business address: _____ ☐ Preferred address

_____

Day phone: _____ Evening phone: _____

Fax line: _____ Cell phone: _____

E-mail address: _____

Okay to leave messages everywhere? _____ If not, explain: _____

_____

Preferred means of communication: _____

Date of birth: _____ Age: _____

Other significant dates: _____

Preferred coaching schedule:

on (day of week) _____ at (time of day) _____

Names of important people in your life (spouse, partner, children, friends, etc.):

_____

_____

Emergency contact: _____

Other information you want me to know (you may continue on back of page):

_____

_____

_____

How did you hear about my coaching services? _____

What influenced your decision to work with a coach?

_____

_____

_____

Have you ever been coached? If so, please describe the experience.

_____

_____

_____

Do you have specific goals for the coaching relationship? If not, what goals might you now create?

_____

_____

_____

_____

_____

What are your significant commitments?

_____

_____

_____

_____

What would your perfect life look like?

_____

_____

_____

_____

_____

# The Welcome Packet

What are your dreams?

_____

_____

_____

What dreams have you given up on?

_____

_____

_____

Where do you want to focus first?

_____

_____

_____

What parts of your life are working best now?

_____

_____

_____

What parts of life are working least well?

_____

_____

_____

What are your values?

_____

_____

_____

What stops you from having the life you want to have?

_____

_____

_____

## YOUR LIFE STORY

Please write in any style you desire and be as creative as you want. Detail any important aspects, accomplishments, and highlights that you feel are important for me to know. **Please send this with a recent picture if we are coaching by phone.**

_____

_____

_____

_____

_____

_____

_____

_____

_____

_____

_____

_____

_____

_____

_____

_____

_____

_____

_____

_____

_____

_____

_____

_____

## *THE FIRST STEP: DE-CLUTTERING*

We put up with, accept, take on, and are dragged down by people and situations that we may have come to ignore in our lives rather than fix. Now is the time to identify those things that drain your energy for positive activities. As you think of more items, add them to your list.

You may or may not choose to do anything about them right now, but just becoming aware of and articulating them will bring them to the forefront, where you'll naturally start eliminating, fixing, or resolving them.

| ENERGY DRAINERS AT WORK | ENERGY DRAINERS AT HOME |
|---|---|
| 1) | 1) |
| 2) | 2) |
| 3) | 3) |
| 4) | 4) |
| 5) | 5) |
| 6) | 6) |
| 7) | 7) |
| 8) | 8) |
| 9) | 9) |
| 10) | 10) |
| 11) | 11) |
| 12) | 12) |
| 13) | 13) |
| 14) | 14) |
| 15) | 15) |
| 16) | 16) |
| 17) | 17) |
| 18) | 18) |
| 19) | 19) |
| 20) | 20) |

# LIFE BALANCE WHEEL
## (Coaching Mandala)

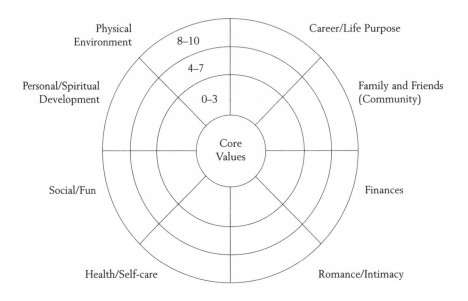

© Patrick Williams, Institute for Life Coach Training

The hub represents your core values—each area interrelated in an ideal life. Give yourself a score (1–10) and shade or color in the space accordingly. Use this Coaching Mandala as a way to assess the level of life satisfaction in each area. You may score it numerically to measure the improvement desired, or you may use it to have a coaching conversation about gaps between where you are now and where you would like to be.

## TEMPLATE FOR PERSONAL VISION STATEMENT

I strongly believe that we are each the creator and director of our own life drama, able to create "on purpose" what our life will look like, feel like, and be like.

It is your opportunity and responsibility to write the script, be the producer and director, and gather the other characters in your life drama. Some people live painful dramas or unfulfilling dramas, but if you are conscious and on purpose with what you want your life to be, it has a much greater chance of evolving into your vision.

So how does one begin designing one's life? First of all you can begin to revisit and remember dreams and desires from your younger years. What drove you? What did you want to become? Who did you admire? Divide your life into thirds and ask yourself what accomplishments or happy events occurred in each third of your life? What values were represented? Are those values still present?

### Exercise: My Personal Vision

Complete the following sentences as though your life were exactly as you would like it to be. Let this be an accurate reflection of what you envision for your **ideal** life. After you have completed all these pieces of your personal vision, you can write a summary paragraph that encapsulates all your intentions, desires, and values.

1. In my family life I am committed to _____
_____.
(spending time with, enjoying, teaching, working with, taking care of) my spouse, partner, friends, family, and/or children.

2. For recreation and fun, I enjoy _____
_____.

3. My home environment will be _____
_____.
(nurturing, comfortable, a place for entertainment, on the water, spacious, have a home office, in the city, in the country, etc.)

4. My retirement home will be _____

_____.

(a cabin in the mountains, a seaside condo, a small restored Victorian home, a large, spacious home to accommodate visiting grandchildren and guests, a large motor home, a houseboat, etc.)

5. My hobbies, passions, interests are _____

_____.

(world travel, politics, reading, writing, sports, gardening, martial arts, etc.)

6. I will maintain (or regain) my health by _____

_____.

(exercising, eating healthy foods, lowering my stress, meditating, etc.)

## Exercise: My Professional Life

1. I will concentrate my practice in the areas of_____

_____.

(fill in with niche or types of clients)

2. My office environment will be _____

_____.

(spacious, comfortable, a home office, efficient, well-organized, etc.)

3. My financial plans are to _____

_____.

(earn a minimum of _____ per year, save 20% of my income, leverage my investments to retire at age _____ with a yearly income of _____ allow for four vacations a year, buy a retirement home, etc.)

4. My business philosophy is one of _____

_____.

(integrity, leadership, dedication to my clients, providing superior coaching and modeling for my clients, being known as an expert in my specialty, etc.)

## *Personal Vision Worksheet*

Using the information you have gathered about yourself in the preceding exercises, write your personal vision in paragraph form. You may do a rough draft and then polish it in the weeks to come.

In my personal life, I am committed to _____

_____.

In my professional life, I am committed to _____

_____.

## GOALS

What goals, aspirations, desires, or intentions do you want to accomplish in the first 6 months of life coaching?

**Business:**

**Personal:**

What do you want to accomplish, change, or create in the first 30 days of life coaching?

**Business:**

**Personal:**

What I hope to gain from this coaching relationship:

Other things I'd like my coach to know about me:

## *SESSION PREPARATION FORM*

Date: _____

To get the most out of your coaching session, it is best to spend several minutes preparing for it. Please e-mail or fax me a copy before your session.

What I have accomplished since our last session—my wins or victories:

☐

☐

☐

What I didn't get done but want to be held accountable for:

☐

☐

☐

Challenges I am facing right now:

☐

☐

☐

What I am appreciative of or grateful/thankful for:

☐

☐

☐

How I want to use my coach today and what I want to get out of this call:

☐

☐

☐

What I commit to doing before the next session:

☐

☐

☐

# References

Adler, A. (1956). *The individual psychology of Alfred Adler: A systematic presentation in selections from his writings.* (H. L. Ansbacher & R. R. Ansbacher, Eds.). New York: Basic Books.

Adler, A. (1998). *Understanding human nature.* (C. Brett, Trans.). Center City, MN: Hazelden. (Original work published 1927)

Albee, G. W. (1998). Fifty years of clinical psychology: Selling our soul to the devil. *Applied and Preventive Psychology, 7,* 189–194. Albee, G. W. (2000, February). The Boulder model's fatal flaw. *American Psychologist, 55*(2), 247–248.

Allport, G. (1937). *Personality: A psychological interpretation.* New York: Holt.

Allport, G. (1955). *Becoming: Basic considerations for a psychology of personality.* New Haven, CT: Yale University Press.

Allport, G. (1961). *Pattern and growth in personality.* New York: Holt, Rinehart & Winston.

Arloski, M. (1994). The ten tenets of wellness. *Wellness Management, 10* (3), 1, 4.

Assagioli, R. (1965). *Psychosynthesis: A manual of principles and techniques.* New York: Hobbs, Dorman.

Bandler, R., & Grindler, J. (1975). *Patterns of the hypnotic techniques of Milton H. Erickson, M.D.* Cupertino, CA: Meta.

Barlow, C. (1998). *Coaching toward excellence: Families and groups*. San Diego: Quest Group.

Berg, I. K. (1994). *Family-based services: A solution-focused approach*. New York: Norton.

Berg, I. K., & Szabo, P. (2005). *Brief coaching for lasting solutions*. New York: Norton.

Bugental, J. F. T. (1967). *Challenges of humanistic psychology*. New York: McGraw-Hill.

Cameron, J. (1992). *The artist's way: A spiritual path to higher creativity*. Los Angeles, CA: Tarcher/Putnam.

Canfield, J., & Hansen, M. V. (1993). *Chicken soup for the soul: 101 stories to open the heart and rekindle the spirit*. Deerfield Beach, FL: Health Communications.

Capner, M., & Caltabiano, M. L. (1993). Factors affecting the progression towards burnout: A comparison of professional and volunteer counselors. *Psychological Reports, 73*, 555–561.

Davis, D., & Humphrey, K. (2000). *College counseling: Issues and strategies for the new millennium*. Alexandria, VA: American Counseling Association.

de Shazer, S. (1985). *Keys to solution in brief therapy*. New York: Norton.

de Shazer, S. (1988). *Clues: Investigating solutions in brief therapy*. New York: Norton.

Drucker, P. F. (1974). *Management: Tasks, responsibilities, practices*. New York: Harper & Row.

Ellis, D. (1998). *Life coaching: A new career for helping professionals*. Rapid City, SD: Breakthrough Enterprises.

Ellis, D. (1999). *Becoming a master student*. Boston: Houghton Mifflin.

Ellis, D. (2000). *Falling awake: Creating the life of your dreams*. Rapid City, SD: Breakthrough Enterprises.

Ellis, D., & Lankowitz, S. (1995). *Human being*. Rapid City, SD: Breakthrough Enterprises.

Erickson, M. H. (1990). *Uncommon casebook: The complete clinical work of Milton H. Erickson*. (W. H. O'Hanlon & A. L. Hexum, Eds.). New York: Norton.

Fadiman, J., & Frager, R. (1976). *Personality and personal growth*. Upper Saddle River, NJ: Harper & Row.

# References

Farber, B. A. (1990). Burnout in psychotherapists: Incidents, types and trends. *Psychotherapy in Private Practice, 8*, 35–44.

Feld, J. (1998). SoHo Success Letter™. E-mail: Judy@CoachNet.com. Website: *www.coachnet.com*. Phone: 972-931-6366.

Figley, C. R. (1993). Compassion stress: Toward its measurement and management. *Family Therapy News*, issue 24.

Fortgang, L. B. (1998). *Take yourself to the top: The secrets of America's #1 career coach*. New York: Warner.

Frankl, V. E. (1959). *Man's search for meaning*. New York: Pocket Books.

Freud, S. (1965). *New introductory lectures on psychoanalysis*. New York: Norton.

Freud, S. (1982). *Basic works of Sigmund Freud*. (J. Strackey, Trans./Ed.). Franklin Center, PA: Franklin Library.

Freudenberger, H. J. (1974). Staff burnout. *Journal of Social Issues, 30*(1), 159–165.

Gilliland, B. E., & James, R. K. (1997). *Crisis intervention strategies*. Pacific Grove: Brooks/Cole.

Goble, F. (1971). *The third force: The psychology of Abraham Maslow*. New York: Simon & Schuster.

Goldberg, M. C. (1998). *The art of the question: A guide to short-term question-centered therapy*. New York: Wiley.

Goldstein, K. (1963). *Human nature in the light of psychopathology*. New York, Schocken.

Gottman, J. M. (1976). *A couple's guide to communication*. Champaign, IL: Research Press.

Gottman, J. M. (1999). *The seven principles for making marriage work*. New York: Crown.

Gottman, J. M., & DeClaire, J. (2001). *The relationship cure: A five-step guide for building better connections with family, friends, and lovers*. New York: Crown.

Gottman, J. M., & Silver, N. (1994). *The seven principles for making marriage work*. New York: Crown.

Haley, J. (1986). *Uncommon therapy: The psychiatric techniques of Milton H. Erickson*. New York: Norton. (Original work published 1973)

Hargrove, R. (1995). *Masterful coaching*. San Diego: Pfeiffer.

Hayden, C. J. (1999). *Get clients now!: A 28-day marketing program for professionals and consultants*. New York: AMACOM.

Hendrix, H. (1988). *Getting the love you want: A guide for couples*. New York: Holt.

Hill, N. (1990). *Think and grow rich*. Los Angeles: Fawcett.

Horney, K. (1980). *The adolescent diaries of Karen Horney*. New York: Basic Books.

Hudson, F. (1999a). *The adult years*. San Francisco: Jossey-Bass.

Hudson, F. (1999b). *The handbook of coaching: A comprehensive resource guide for managers, executives, consultants, and human resource professionals*. San Francisco: Jossey-Bass.

Ivey, A. E. (1994). *Intentional interviewing and counseling: Facilitating client development in a multicultural society*. Pacific Grove, CA: Brooks.

Jourard, S. M. (1974). *Healthy personality: An approach from the viewpoint of humanistic psychology*. New York: Macmillan.

Jung, C. G. (1933). *Modern man in search of a soul*. London: Trubner.

Jung, C. G. (1953). *The collected works of C. G. Jung*. (H. Read, M. Fordham, & G. Adler, Eds.). New York: Pantheon.

Jung, C. G. (1970). *Civilization in transition*. (R. F. C. Hull, Trans.). Princeton, NJ: Princeton University Press.

Jung, C. G. (1976). *The portable Jung*. (J. Campbell, Ed.; R. F. C. Hull, Trans.). New York: Penguin Books.

Kesey, K. (1962). *One flew over the cuckoo's nest*. New York: Viking.

Klein, H. (2000, October). Practice building: The coaching phenomenon marches on. *Psychotherapy Finances, 26*(7), 5–7.

Lecky, P. (1945). Self-consistency: *A theory of personality*. New York: Island Press.

Leonard, T. (1998). *The portable coach*. New York: Scribner.

Lewin, K. (1935). *A dynamic theory of personality*. New York: McGraw-Hill.

Lewin, K. (1938). *The conceptual representation and the measurement of psychological forces*. Durham, NC: Duke University Press.

Lowry, S., & Menendez, D. (1997). *Discovering your best self through the art of coaching*. Houston: NexusPoint/Enterprise.

Madanes, C. (1981). *Strategic family therapy*. San Francisco: Jossey-Bass.

# References

Madanes, C. (1984). *Behind the one-way mirror: Advances in the practice of strategic therapy*. San Francisco: Jossey-Bass.

Maslach, C. (1982). *Burnout: The cost of caring*. Englewood Cliffs, NJ: Prentice-Hall.

Maslow, A. (1987). *Motivation and personality*. New York: Harper. (Original work published 1954)

Maslow, A. (1962). *Toward a psychology of being*. Princeton, NJ: Van Nostrand.

Maslow, A. (1993). *Farther reaches of human nature*. New York: Arkana.

May, R. (1953). *Man's search for himself*. New York: Norton.

May, R. (1975). *The courage to create*. New York: Norton.

May, R. (1979). *Psychology and the human dilemma*. New York: Norton.

McGraw, P. (1999). *Life strategies: Doing what works, doing what matters*. New York: Hyperion.

Myers, J. E. (1991). Wellness as the paradigm for counseling and development: The possible future. *Counselor Education and Supervision, 30,* 183–193.

O'Hanlon, B. (1999a). *Do one thing different*. New York: Morrow.

O'Hanlon, B. (1999b). *Guide to possibility land*. New York: Norton.

O'Hanlon, W. H., & Martin, M. (1992). *Solution-oriented hypnosis: An Ericksonian approach*. New York: Norton.

Perls, F. S. (1966). Ego, hunger and aggression: A revision of Freud's theory and method. San Francisco: Orbit Graphics Arts.

Perls, F. S. (1973). *The Gestalt approach and eye witness to therapy*. Ben Lomand, CA: Science & Behavior.

Phillips, B. (1999). *Body for life*. New York: HarperCollins.

Prather, H. (1970). *Notes to myself*. Moab, UT: Real People Press.

Richardson, C. (1998). *Take time for your life: A personal coach's seven step program for creating the life you want*. New York: Broadway.

Richardson, C. (2000). *Life makeovers*. New York: Broadway.

Ries, L., & Ries, A. (1998). *The 22 immutable laws of branding*. New York: HarperBusiness.

Rilke, R. M. (1904). *Letters to a young poet*. (M. D. Herter, Trans.). New York: Norton.

Rogers, C. (1951). *Client-centered therapy*. Boston: Houghton Mifflin.

Satir, V. (1964). *Conjoint family therapy: A guide to therapy and techniques*. Palo Alto, CA: Science & Behavior.

Satir, V. (1976). *Making contact*. Millbrae, CA: Celestial Arts.

Satir, V. (1991). *Satir model: Family therapy and beyond*. Palo Alto, CA: Science & Behavior.

Satir, V., & Baldiwin, M. (1983). *Step by step: A guide to creating change in families*. Palo Alto, CA: Science & Behavior.

Schaufeli, W. B., Maslach, C., & Marek, T. (Eds.). (1993). *Professional burnout: Recent developments in theory and research*. Washington, DC: Taylor & Francis.

Schneider, K. J., Bugental, J. F. T., & Pierson, J. F. (Eds.). (2002). *The handbook of humanistic psychology*. Thousand Oaks, CA: Sage.

Steele, D. (1997). *Professional coaching and the marriage and family therapist*. California Therapist, 12(2), 54–55.

Toffler, A. (1970). *Future shock*. New York: Bantam Books.

Walter, J., & Peller, J. (2000). *Recreating brief therapy: Preferences and possibilities*. New York: Norton.

Weiner-Davis, M. (1992). *Divorce busting: A revolutionary and rapid program for staying together*. New York: Summit.

Whitmore, J. (1995). *Coaching for performance*. Sonoma, CA: Nicholas Brealey.

Whitworth, L., Kimsey-House, H., & Sandahl, P. (1998). *Co-active coaching*. Palo Alto, CA: Davies-Black.

Williams, P. (1980). *Transpersonal psychology: An introductory guidebook*. Greeley, CO: Lutey.

Williams, P. (1997). Telephone coaching for cash draws new client market. *Practice Strategies, 2*, 11.

Williams, P. (1999). The therapist as personal coach: Reclaiming your soul! *The Independent Practitioner, 19*(4), 204–207.

Williams, P. (2000a, June). Personal coaching's evolution from therapy. *Consulting Today* [Special issue], 4.

Williams, P. (2000b, July). Practice building: The coaching phenomenon marches on. *Psychotherapy Finances, 26*(315), 1–2.

# References

Williams, P. (2004a) Coaching evolution and revolution: The history, development, ans distinctions that will define coaching as the most important organizational development of the future. *Absolute Advantage, 3*(4), 6–9.

Williams, P. (2004b) Coaching versus psychotherapy: The great debate. *Choice Magazine, 2*(1), 38–39.

Williams, P., & Menendez D. (2007). *Becoming a professional life coach: Lessons from the Institute for Life Coach Training*. New York: Norton.

Williams, P., Anderson, S. (Eds). (2005). *The law and ethics of coaching*. Hoboken: Wiley Books.

Williams, P. & Thomas, L. (2005). *Total life coaching*. New York: Norton.

Zieg, J. K. (1994). *Ericksonian methods: The essence of the story*. New York: Brunner/Mazel.

# Index

# Index

# Index